STAGE FRIGHT

HEALTH & SAFETY IN THE THEATER

Monona Rossol, M.S., M.F.A., I.H.

D0680657

ALLWORTH PRESS, NEW YORK
Copublished with the American Council for the Arts

© 1986, 1991 by Monona Rossol

Published by Allworth Press, an imprint of Allworth Communications, Inc.,
10 East 23rd Street, New York, NY 10010

Distributor to the trade in the United States:
Consortium Book Sales & Distribution, Inc.,
287 East Sixth Street, Suite 365, Saint Paul, MN 55101

Distributor to the trade in Canada:
Raincoast Books Distribution Limited, 112 East 3rd Avenue, Vancouver, B.C. V5T 1C8

Library of Congress Catalog Card Number: 90-85553

ISBN: 0-9607118-3-X

Table 10, page 99: from *Consumer Guide to Cosmetics* by Tom Conry. Copyright © 1979, 1980 by Science Action Coalition. Reprinted by permission of Doubleday & Company, Inc.

Table 11, page 101: reproduced from *Cosmetics and Toiletries* by permission of Allured Publishing.

Tables 14, 15; pages 114, 115: This material is reproduced with permission from American National Standard Practice for Occupational and Educational Eye and Face Protection, ANSI Z87.1-1979, copyright © 1979 by the American National Standards Institute, copies of which may be purchased from the American National Standards Institute at 1430 Broadway, New York, New York 10018.

Figures 2, 4, 5; pages 45, 49, 66: Sedonia Champlain

Cartoons: Lorna L. Bosnos

Design model: Bruce McPherson

Cover design: Douglas Design Associates, New York

This book was written to provide the most current and accurate information about health and safety standards in the theatre and about applicable laws and regulations. However, the author and publisher can take no responsibility for any harm or damage that might be caused by the use or misuse of any information contained herein. It is not the purpose of this book to provide medical diagnosis, suggest health treatment, or provide legal or regulatory counseling. Readers should seek advice from physicians, safety professionals, industrial hygienists, environmental health specialists, and attorneys concerning specific problems.

Contents

Foreword

Monona Rossol is not a stranger either to theater, the sciences, or the health and safety field. When she was a year old, she was being produced as a magician's prop out of a series of neatly fitted boxes. By the age of three, she was a professional acrobat in vaudeville, a facet of her stage career that was stopped short by a dramatic face-down somersault on an outdoor cement stage when she was fourteen. She then turned her attention to singing and acting theatrically, performing in operas, plays, and musicals throughout Wisconsin and New York, including stints with the Wisconsin Idea Theater, Badger Ballads, Madison Civic Opera, All Souls Players in New York, and "Reunion" at Playwrights' Horizons Off Broadway. She has also developed a highly successful cabaret act in which she sings early show music.

Monona received her bachelor's degree with honors in chemistry and mathematics at the University of Wisconsin, with special emphasis in pre-medical courses. Then in graduate school she turned her attention to art, especially ceramics, glassblowing, and sculpture. By the late 1950's and early 1960's she was well aware that many art departments operated under less than healthy conditions when her classmates undertook such reckless activities as firing hydrochloric acid-emitting ceramic salt kilns indoors without so much as a word of caution from the academic staff. Such experiences prompted her to practice safer techniques in her own studios and classrooms, and to warn her students, young and old, about health hazards.

In the sciences, Monona was regularly employed during undergraduate and graduate school as a research chemist in both academic and commercial chemical laboratories. In January 1977, together with Michael McCann and Catherine Jenkins, Monona helped to incorporate the Center for Occupational Hazards, with which she was associated until 1987. She then founded ACTS (Arts, Crafts and Theater Safety), for which she continues to write, consult, and lecture about health and safety in the arts. This book is a culmination of her lifelong concern for, and love of, theater.

John O. Holzhueter

Preface

If this were, as Candide believed, the best of all possible worlds, this book would not be necessary. Ideally, everyone involved with the theater—amateurs and professionals alike—would know everything in this book.

Much of the basic theater health and safety information that follows, however, will be new to many. For decades, theater students and apprentices have worked in schools and shops that lacked proper ventilation and protective devices. They rarely have been instructed about the toxicity of materials, the hazards of particular tasks, the laws and regulations that apply to their work, or getting help from governmental and private agencies. Some of these students are now working professionals engaged in teaching others, so the cycle continues.

To break the cycle and remediate the shortcomings will be difficult. Information that should have been delivered in easily digestible bits throughout years of schooling now must be swallowed in large chunks. Much of the information seems technical and unpalatable—and many people in theater fled from mathematics, physics, and chemistry in school. Unfortunately, I could not avoid scientific and technical information, but have tried instead to treat each subject as succinctly as possible.

To make the best use of this manual, begin with the chapters about the basics. The most critical ones are "Safety and Health in Theater" and "Health Hazards." You need to know, for example, what makes some chemicals harmful, how they enter the body, and what illnesses they can cause before you can evaluate the hazards of the products you are using. If your work requires any kind of ventilation or respiratory protection, add those chapters to the critical list.

Only the most important facts could be covered in this book, and I hope many readers will pursue additional readings on pertinent topics. Acquiring theater health and safety information should be an ongoing process, just as keeping abreast of technical theater information is automatic for backstage artists or reading and seeing new plays is a compulsion for actors and directors.

Theater safety means more than just looking up the hazards of your specific product in a reference book. Even if a volume listing the thousands of products used in theater could be created, it would soon be out of date: products' compositions change, and new items are added to the list almost daily. It is far better to show you how to research products on your own, and this book takes you through the important first steps.

I welcome your further inquiries and wish you all the best. But in the interest of health and safety, don't break a leg.

M. R.

Acknowledgments

A grant from the Theater Program of the New York State Council on the Arts has made this book possible. Actor's Equity Foundation, Inc. provided additional funding as did many individuals from all phases of theater, including those who responded to a fund-raising letter signed by Ming Cho Lee.

Michael McCann, my associate at the Center for Occupational Hazards, acted as consultant and critical reader, Devora Neumark coordinated production, and the rest of the staff, especially Perri Peltz, lightened my work load whenever possible so that I could bring this work to completion. John O. Holzhueter edited, rewrote, and endured my two-year preoccupation with this project. Eric Gertner, a member of our board—and of too many theater organizations to enumerate—provided bibliographic, electrical, and lighting expertise, and was always on call.

Many others should be acknowledged, including Randy Davidson and Don Calvert, Commissioner and Vice-Commissioner, respectively, of Health and Safety for the United States Institute of Theater Technology, for their well-known pioneering interest in the field. Barbara Pook and Tony Diemont deserve thanks for advice, especially on rigging. Dr. Jacqueline Messite and especially her colleague Nick Fannick of NIOSH Region II helped with the section on fog and smoke—a subject as clouded as its name implies.

Others who deserve individual thanks are Michel Kinter and Paul Eden, Business Representative and member of Actor's Equity Foundation, Inc., respectively; Alida Dressler and Parmelee Welles of the United Scenic Artists; Liz Argo Clark of the National Association of Broadcasters and Electrical Technicians; and Frank Mayfield, Technical Director at Niles North High School in Skokie, Illinois, who shared his knowledge of high school theatrical hazards.

Update

STAGE FRIGHT was first published in 1986. Since then, important changes have taken place about which you should know. Fortunately, we are printing a new edition in January 1991 so I can make you aware of the following changes:

1. Right-to-know (or hazard communication) provisions of the occupational safety and health regulations in both the United States and Canada have been extended to include all workplaces, including theaters and schools (which updates the information on page 36.) This means that many of the suggestions in STAGE FRIGHT (pages 31-38) are now mandated by law. In fact, STAGE FRIGHT may be used as a text for the required right-to-know training programs.

2. The United States federal art materials labeling law mentioned on page 33 was passed in October of 1988. It amends the Federal Hazardous Substances Act to provide chronic hazard labeling for art materials and to ban toxic materials from use by children in grade six and under. Readers can expect to see the law in force in 1991.

3. Many of the air quality standards (Threshold Limit Values and OSHA Permissible Exposure Limits) have changed. In all cases they were lowered to more stringent limits.

4. The Center for Occupational Hazards, referred to throughout the book, has changed its name to the Center for Safety in the Arts (CSA). And a new organization, Arts, Crafts and Theater Safety (ACTS), has been formed which provides similar services.

Of these changes, the most significant for readers are the changes in the workplace regulations. The following section should be considered as an update to all regulatory information in the text.

LAWS PROTECTING THEATER WORKERS

Both the United States and Canada have very complex regulations governing the relationship between employer and employee. However, whether the regulations are called the Occupational Safety and Health Act (OSHAct in the United States) or Occupational Health and Safety Act (OHSAct in Canada), their main purpose is very simple — to protect workers.

The OSHAct general duty clause reads in part that the "employer shall furnish...employment and a place of employment which are free from recognized hazards." The Canadian OHSAct requires' employers and supervisors to ``take every precaution reasonable in the circumstances for the protection of a worker.''

These brief general statements serve as the foundation for complex regulatory structures. The regulations address chemical exposures, noise, ladder safety, machinery guarding and a host of subjects. And many of these rules apply to theaters, shops and schools. A copy of these general industry standards can be obtained from federal, state or provincial departments of labor and should be kept handy for reference.

RIGHT-TO-KNOW OR HAZARDS COMMUNICATION RULES

Among the workplace regulations are the recently instituted "right-to-know" laws. United States right-to-know laws were first passed by a number of states. Then a similar federal regulation called the OSHA Hazard Communication Standard (sometimes called the federal right-to-know law) was instituted in 1988. The result is that almost all employees in the United States now are covered by one or the other (sometimes both) of these laws. Even federal workers, so long exempt from OSHA regulations, come under this rule.

There is a similar history in Canada with the resulting passage of the federal Workplace Hazardous Materials Information System (WHMIS).

CITATIONS, FINES AND LEGAL ACTIONS

Penalties and fines can be levied in both the United States and Canada for infractions of any of the occupational safety and health laws. However, fines in the United States now can be large enough to threaten the existence of the company.

A sevenfold increase in the schedule of some OSHA penalties is one provision of the five-year deficit reduction package signed in 1990 by President Bush. For example, the maximum penalties for safety and health violations were raised from $1,000 to $7,000 per violation. In addition, the measure established a new minimum penalty of $5,000 for each willful violation and raised the allowable civil penalty for each willful or repeat violation from $10,000 to $70,000.

Another Force driving compliance with the regulations is personal and criminal liability for corporate managers. Once protected by worker's compensation laws, employers in the United States now can be sued for illnesses and accidents arising from deliberate or knowing violations of the regulations. In the United States there are employers serving prison time for violating health and safety laws.

RIGHT-TO-KNOW COMPLIANCE

Today, OSHA gives more citations for hazard communication violations than for any other rule infraction. Once a theater is cited, budgets and schedules must be completely revised to make compliance its first priority. I have personally participated in program development and training in several cited theaters and shops. One was a Broadway theater company cited under New York State's right-to-know law.

Clearly, it is far better to set up right-to-know programs before being cited. Yet many theaters, shops and schools still do not comply. This is partly due to ignorance of the law's existence and partly to a mistaken belief that many laws do not apply to theater — that we are somehow "special."

Some small companies also resist compliance because they feel the cost is too high. These complaints really reflect our difficulty in facing the fact that for far too many years we have spent far too little on health and safety.

RIGHT-TO-KNOW PROVISIONS

In general, both United States and Canadian laws require employers to develop formal hazard communication programs, provide employees access to complete inventories and data sheets for all potentially hazardous chemicals in the workplace, and set up formal training programs for all employees who potentially are exposed to toxic chemicals.

Examples of materials which must be included in the program are paints, dyes, solvents, metals, cleaning materials, and special effects smoke and pyrotechnics. Craftspeople, technicians, performers and all others who are exposed to such materials must be informed and trained.

Actually, the law requires what common sense should have dictated years ago. Workers should not be asked to use or breathe chemicals about which they are not fully informed and trained.

Instead, theaters often are full of people who think they understand the hazards of their materials when they have only read the labels. Such people endanger themselves and others. Labels provide only brief warnings which must be combined with a great deal of other information in order to protect workers.

If this law had been instituted earlier, many occupational illnesses and allergies among theater workers and performers would have been prevented.

WHO'S COVERED?

Almost all employees in the United States are covered by state or federal hazard communication (Hazard Communications) laws. Exempted are some state and municipal employees in states that do not have an accepted state OSHA plan. All employees in Canada are covered by the Workplace Hazardous Materials Information System (WHMIS). (The employer is the person or entity that takes the deductions out of the paycheck.)

Self-employed or independent contractors are not covered, but they may be affected by the laws. For example, if you work as an independent contractor at a theater or shop where there are employees, all the products and materials you bring onto the premises must conform to the employer's right-to-know or Workplace Hazardous Materials Information System program labeling requirements. Your use of these products also must conform

TEACHER'S LIABILITY

Teachers have a unique obligation arising from the fact that they can be held liable for any harm classroom activities cause their students. To protect against liability, teachers should formally transmit to students right-to-know training about the dangers of classroom materials and processes. They also must enforce the safety rules and act as good examples by taking proper precautions.

Theater schools and universities should be in the forefront of this movement. They should encourage teachers and students to explore safer media, find substitutes for toxic materials, and research and develop alternatives to hazardous processes. Schools that teach theater arts and crafts also must develop curricula which include formal right-to-know health and safety training.

COMPLYING WITH RIGHT-TO-KNOW LAWS

To comply, first find out which law applies to you. Call your local department of labor and ask them whether you must comply with a state/provincial or federal right-to-know law.

Ask for a copy of the law which applies to you. Also ask for explanatory materials. Some of the government agencies have prepared well-written guidelines to take you through compliance step by step. Two good sources of such guidance are:

Hazard Communication: A Compliance Kit, U.S. Department of Labor, OSHA publication 3104. For sale by the Superintendent of Documents, U.S. Government Printing Office, Washington, DC 20402

WHMIS Core Material: A Resource Manual for the Application and Implementation of WHMIS. Contact the Community Relations Department, Worker's Compensation Board of British Columbia, 6951 Westminster Highway, Richmond, BC V7C 1C6 Cananda

GENERAL REQUIREMENTS OF RIGHT-TO-KNOW LAWS

There are small differences between the United States and Canadian laws. For example, the definition of "hazardous" varies, and the Canadian law requires information in French. However, the two laws require employers to take similar steps toward compliance:

1. Inventory all workplace chemicals. Even products such as bleach and cleaning materials may qualify as hazardous products. List everything. (This is an excellent time to cut down paper work by trimming your inventory. Dispose of old, unneeded or seldom-used products.)

2. Identify hazardous products in your inventory. Apply the definition of "hazardous" in the right-to-know law which applies to you.

3. Assemble Material Safety Data Sheets (MSDSs) on all hazardous products. Write to manufacturers, distributors and importers of all products on hand for MSDSs. Require MSDSs as a condition of purchase for all new materials.

4. Check all product labels to be sure they comply with the law's labeling requirements. Products which do not comply must be eliminated or relabeled.

5. Prepare and apply proper labels to all containers into which chemicals have been transferred. (Chemicals in unlabeled containers that are used up within one shift need not be labeled.)

6. Consult Material Safety Data Sheets to identify all operations which use or generate hazardous materials. Be aware that nonhazardous materials when chemically reacted, heated or burned may produce toxic emissions.

7. Make all lists of hazardous materials, Material Safety Data Sheets, and other required written materials available to employees. (The OSHA Hazard Communications Standard and some state right-to-know laws also require a written program which details all these procedures.)

8. Implement a training program.

TRAINING

All employees in both the United States and Canada already should have received right-to-know training. Additional training should take place whenever new employees are hired or new materials or processes introduced. Some state laws require yearly retraining as well. WHMIS requires a yearly review of the training program and retraining if the review indicates it is needed.

The amount of time the training should take is not specified. This is because the law intends the training requirements to be performance oriented — that is, the employees must be given whatever information they need to understand the hazards of their specific jobs and how to work safely. Often short quizzes are used to verify that the employees have understood the presentation.

Training for theater artists, craftspeople, performers and teachers usually can be accomplished in a full day. The information which must be communicated includes:

1. The details of the hazard communication program that the employer is conducting, including an explanation of the labeling system, the Material Safety Data Sheets and how employees can obtain and use hazard information.

2. Information and education about the physical and health hazards of the chemicals in the work area. This should include an explanation of *safety hazards* such as fire and explosions, and *health hazards* such as how the chemical enters the body and both the immediate and long-term effects of exposure.

3. Training employees how to protect themselves. This should include safe work practices, emergency procedures, use of personal protective equipment that the employer provides, and an explanation of the ventilation system and other engineering controls that reduce exposure.

4. Teaching employees how the presence of hazardous chemicals can be detected in the work area. This should include training about environmental and medical monitoring conducted by the employer, use of monitoring devices, the visual appearance and odor of chemicals and any other detection or warning methods.

This book can be used to address points 2 through 4 above, providing employers, employees and teachers with formal training materials.

For advice about right-to-know or other health and safety matters, readers are encouraged to call or write: Monona Rossol, ACTS (Arts, Crafts and Theater Safety, Inc.) 181 Thompson Street, # 23, New York, NY 10012 • 212-777-0062

I

Before you begin

Safety and health in theater

Safety hazards

It would be hard to imagine an industry with more hazards than theater. Actors act, ignoring the ten- or fifteen-foot drop into the orchestra pit a few inches away. Fire, smoke, and explosions occur on stage. Split-second scene changes take place in the dark. Peter Pan soars overhead on a thin line.

Many theater professionals, on the other hand, tend to take these risks for granted. They would prefer no interference; in their opinion, theater safety should be discussed discreetly among themselves.

Unfortunately, only after accidents are reported is theater safety openly debated in the press—or litigated. But when public attention wanes, the accidents' causes can remain essentially unchanged. Altering this pattern will require open discussion of safety hazards, and formal safety education programs.

Health hazards

Accidents demonstrate that *safety* hazards really do exist, but *health* hazards are less obvious and harder to prove. Health hazards in theater, like industrial health hazards, result when individuals are exposed to toxic chemicals, gases, vapors, fumes, and dusts, or to physical phenomena such as ultraviolet, infrared, and other forms of radiant energy; noise; vibration; and excessive heat and cold.

Intensive exposure to one of these health hazards quickly may result in a serious illness or even death. However, it is more likely that repeated small exposures over weeks, months, or years will affect individuals gradually. Often by the time an illness manifests itself, the damage is serious, sometimes even irreversible. A number of commonly accepted theatrical practices, attitudes, and conditions place actors and technicians in greater jeopardy than they would be even in many factory jobs.

Causes of exposure to hazards

Haste: It doesn't have to be safe, it has to be Tuesday. Rarely, if ever, does any theater allow enough time for any phase of production to be planned and executed. Time spent doing things carefully and safely isn't visible to the audience, while time spent on a special effect or a new backdrop is. But it really is shortsighted not to take the time to do a thing right the first time because somehow there is always time to do it over.

Unsafe conditions: jury rig, make do, and hope it holds. Many theaters and shops have bad ventilation systems; unsafe walking surfaces and stairs; outdated, poorly maintained, or unguarded saws and other equipment; poor work lighting; and recycled scenery and rickety props.

Unsafe theaters should be repaired or go dark. Unsafe equipment should be repaired, replaced, or taken out of service. Productions and theater activities should be planned around a facility's limitations. For example, only shops equipped with spray booths should do spray painting; shows should be staged with only limited amounts of scenery, props, or lighting effects if doing otherwise means using unsafe equipment.

Bad attitudes

Macho: Alive, well, and living in the theater. Performers and technicians alike commonly believe that suffering, risk-taking, and even dying for art is an appropriate price to pay for the privilege of working in the field. Actors say, "The show must go on." But theater arts should not be seen as the equivalent of wilderness survival expeditions. Theatrical amateurs and professionals are charged with enlightening and enriching audiences and themselves, not risking life and limb or both. When an effect or stunt is associated with a risk, the risk must be carefully assessed. For instance, risks a professional performer takes must be minimal, calculated, and limited to a minor adverse consequence at worst. Risks to young student performers or to audiences are not acceptable at all.

Horseplay: Only for horses and similar animals. It is not an appropriate way to break rehearsal tension or keep up team spirit. Horseplay causes many injuries and accidents, especially in school theatrical productions. Teachers are expected to have their students under control and they may find themselves liable for accidents caused by reckless behavior.

Lawlessness: Rules and regs are for other folk. Some people believe that theater is exempt from regulations and laws because theater is "special." This idea is encouraged by the fact that authorities fail to monitor and inspect many theaters for compliance with health and safety regulations. Retribution comes when an accident, fire, or other incident occurs, bringing the theater to the authorities' attention. The liabilities or penalties resulting from ignoring the rules usually more than cancel any benefits.

Impaired judgment

Drugs and alcohol: The Barrymore mystique. You have to keep your wits about you in theater, yet many choose to impair their wits by using drugs or alcohol. Just as these chemicals cause accidents on the highway, so too are they responsible for accidents in theater.

Chemicals in products: The hidden enemy. Besides alcohol and street drugs, other chemicals can cause narcosis and impaired judgment. You may inhale these inadvertently while working with paints, costume-cleaning solvents, aerosol spray products, and the like. No one who works in the theater should have these chemicals in their blood stream from either accidental or intentional inhalation.

Medications. Some people take prescription medication that may impair their judgment or that may interact with chemicals they inhale while using paints and other products. People who must use such medication should check with their doctors about possible negative effects. They also should know whether their medications will influence their ability to operate dangerous machinery, drive, or do other hazardous jobs. Teachers should know about their students' physical condition and limitations before assigning tasks.

Lack of sleep or food: We'll stop when we drop. People often try to compensate for insufficient production time by working hours of overtime and skipping meals. In school or community theater, long hours amount to a kind of endurance test given to new volunteers to see if they can take it or to prove they are sufficiently dedicated. Such misplaced enthusiasm among students and amateurs may cause them to work overlong. Whatever the reason, there is no question that long hours and lack of proper nourishment impair judgment and awareness: they can and do cause accidents.

Psychological stress. By its nature, the theater is a difficult environment rife with personal and artistic pressures. However, when a tyrannical director or unreasonable job insecurity, for example, are added to personal and artistic pressures, stresses may be created that can hamper productions and contribute to poor judgments and accidents.

Lack of training: I'll try anything once. When makeup, costume design, scene- and prop-making, and other crafts are taught in schools, teachers rarely alert students to occupational hazards indicated by evidence from studies of related industries. For example, high rates of lung and skin diseases among cosmetologists are associated with sprays, cosmetics, and similar products; makeup artists in theater are exposed to similar products and should beware the health effects. Students of all theatrical crafts should be taught how to evaluate the hazards of the products they use, and how to choose the safest ones, and how to protect themselves from those they do use.

Welding provides another example. In other industries, welders are trained formally and they are required to pass qualifying tests that include welding safety information. But in school theater shops, untrained welders, or those who learned by watching others, do most welding work.

Teachers and theater workers tend to appropriate new and different technologies, so their work appears to be abreast of current trends. Lasers, holography, pyrotechnics, fog and smoke effects, industrial plastics, paints, dyes, and more find their way into the theater. Often the people using these materials or processes have not had sufficient training to know what can go wrong, what to do if something does go wrong, what laws and regulations may apply, and the like.

Theater health and safety training sufficient to correct these shortcomings cannot be relegated to a single lecture or to individual instruction when a particular need arises. Instead, the entire subject requires a thorough and professional approach.

Solutions

Planning. The first step in solving theater *health* problems is to take the time to reexamine how you work and what materials you use. Do not assume a process is safe because it always has been done that way or because no one has become sick or had an accident so far. Instead, investigate the chemical composition of your materials and see that required ventilation exists and that proper protective equipment is available.

The first step in solving theater *safety* problems begins by accepting the validity of Murphy's Law: if something can go wrong, it will. So during the working day, plan ways to respond to foreseeable accidents. For instance, think about the last job you did. Now imagine that a fire had started, or someone nearby received an electric shock or fell. What would you have done first? second? third?

Often, when people are given time to think about questions like this in advance, they make excellent decisions—decisions with which even experts will agree. But when you must respond to such situations without prior preparation, you and nearly everyone else are much more likely to act inappropriately, even harmfully.

After you have begun planning ahead, keep improving your ideas by discussing your plans with peers and experts, by joining and sharing safety information within professional societies and unions, by continuing to learn more about your work, and by using the resources of the federal, state, and local agencies that regulate your workplace.

OSHA: A solution or a problem?

Some of the most violent debates heard in the professional theatrical community concern the rules and regulations of the Occupational Safety and Health Administration (OSHA). A novice, listening to these arguments, would find it difficult to decide if OSHA were a bureaucracy, a destroyer of artistic freedom, or a valuable resource. Clearly, some sensible discussion about OSHA is in order.

What is OSHA? The Occupational Safety and Health Administration was created to carry out the mandate of the Occupational Safety and Health Act of 1970. This act's general-duty clause states that each employer "shall furnish to each of his employees employment and a place of employment which are free from recognized hazards. . . ." To accomplish this, OSHA sets legally enforceable minimum standards for workplace safety and health. Employers bear the responsibility of familiarizing themselves with the standards applicable to their establishments and of making sure that employees have and use all the personal protective gear and equipment required for safety. Even in cases where OSHA has not promulgated specific standards, employers are responsible for following the intent of the act's general-duty clause.

Is your school or theater covered? In the same way that a factory is obliged by law to meet certain minimum safety and health standards, so too are colleges, universities, schools, theaters, and theater shops. All private institutions and many public ones are covered either by a state OSH plan or by the federal OSH Act. Even if your institution is not covered by law, failure to comply with these minimum standards can drastically affect an institution's liability if an accident results in litigation. Be sure you know in which of these ways OSHA affects your school or theater.

Are you covered? The OSH Act applies to employers and employees. Members of other groups—such as students, interns, work-study students, volunteers, and the self-employed—are not covered, but some have the right to sue if they are harmed. Students, for instance, can sue for damages if teachers fail to instruct them about hazards, fail to supervise a student's work, or if hazardous conditions in the theater or shops contribute to an injury. In court, the OSHA standards may be used to determine if hazardous conditions existed.

The standards. The standards that apply to theaters and shops are found in the *General Industry Standards*. This volume is available from your nearest OSHA office. (Look in the telephone directory under U.S. Department of Labor.) These standards are not easy reading and will require study and, occasionally, some informed interpretation. Both state and federal OSHA staffs are helpful in answering questions about compliance.

The portions of the standard that are most applicable to theater pertain to walking and working surfaces, means of egress, medical and first aid, fire protection, machine guards, hand tools and portable power tools, welding equipment, electrical service, occupational health and environmental control (ventilation, noise, etc.), and toxic and hazardous substances. The section on toxic and hazardous substances sets miminum standards for air contaminants such as vapors from solvents found in paints and cleaners, dusts (such as sawdust), and fumes (such as those from welding). Many theater-shop supervisors or owners are not aware that the law requires them to monitor and keep airborne substances below certain concentrations.

Inspections. An employee in institutions under federal OSHA jurisdiction has the right to request an inspection when he or she feels in imminent danger from a hazard or that OSHA standards are being violated. OSHA will inform the employee about any action taken on the complaint. If OSHA decides not to inspect, the employee can request and receive an informal review about the decision. The employee's name will be withheld from the employer if the employee requests it.

Employees and teachers subject to state OSH plans should check with their state offices about complaint procedures. Students and self-employed persons cannot call for inspections.

Employers may take advantage of free on-site consultations provided by state governments or private contractors with funding from OSHA. The state consultant conducts an inspection similar to OSHA's and makes recommendations for corrections of any health and safety hazards. This program is separate from OSHA's inspection program, is confidential, and issues no citations or penalties. At the end of this book is an explanation of how to contact state consultation services.

Variances. OSHA may grant variances to theater owners and managers if safety standards cannot be applied to certain situations, such as trap doors, or unguarded elevators used to raise scenery or choirs. If proper application is made, the variances will be given, allowing the theaters to remain in compliance.

Other OSHA Provisions. There are many other services offered by state and federal OSHAs. Here are some about which theater employees and employers should keep themselves informed.

NIOSH

The National Institute for Occupational Safety and Health also provides services for theater workers. They include:

Health Hazard Evaluations of theaters and shops for hazards. These investigations must be requested by an employer or an authorized representative of a theater's employees, meaning someone who has been authorized in writing by as few as two other employees. If the workplace employs less than four workers, any one of the workers may request a Health Hazard Evaluation. If requested, the name or names of the persons who request the investigation will be kept confidential.

Answering written and telephone requests for information about workplace hazards and toxic materials. For example, in New York, NIOSH (Region II) investigated some brands of artificial fog at the request of Actor's Equity Association.

Answering questions about personal protective equipment, such as respirators;

testing and certifying respiratory protection equipment; researching and developing criteria for recommendations of exposure limits to hazardous chemicals; and developing methods to evaluate workplace hazards, such as air sampling methods.

Publishing and distributing educational and technical information. For further information about their publications and services, contact your nearest NIOSH office.

Other regulators.

Colleges, schools, theaters, and shops are subject to regulation by many additional sources: local and state fire safety laws; building and construction codes; sanitation codes and standards; and state, local, and federal environmental protection laws. An institution's insurance carrier also may have rules and requirements about safety and health hazards, and these may affect a theater's or school's premium costs or coverage.

The complexities of these requirements underscore the need to allocate time for planning and reviewing compliance, for cooperative effort among employees and employers, and for a formal health and safety program in your theater, school, or shop.

Some of these regulators are also sources of free services. For example, most fire departments will advise you about fire safety, and fire department employees are available to teach proper use of fire extinguishers. Large insurance companies also usually employ or retain industrial hygienists and safety experts who will survey facilities free of charge. Implementing insurance companies' suggestions often results in lower premiums.

Health and safety programs

NIOSH and OSHA recommend formal health and safety programs for institutions of all types. If your theater, shop, or school does not have a formal program, you may use one designed for industrial, business, and educational environments. For example, a program in the NIOSH/OSHA training manual *Safety and Health for Industrial/Vocational Education* is easily adapted for use in most theater schools and shops.

The major elements of a formal health and safety program for theaters, schools, and shops are:

administrative responsibility;

recognition and control of hazards;

education and training of personnel;

medical screening and surveillance;

reporting and investigation of accidents, incidents, and illnesses; and

monitoring and evaluating the program

Responsibility for the health and safety program belongs in the hands of a top administrative official, such as a director of a non-profit theater, a dean of a college, or the chairman of a university theater department.

Health and safety committees

Forming a health and safety committee (HSC) is one of the most effective ways to develop and maintain a health and safety program. Members of this committee should be chosen from all levels and all employment areas in your theater or shop. In a theater, for example, you should include actors, lighting technicians, wardrobe attendants, ticket takers, administrators, maintenance workers—at least one person from each job category in your organization. If the theater is unionized, HSC members also should be members of their union HSC or should report directly to the union HSC.

As its first task, the HSC should establish its own procedures and duties using the guidelines in an OSHA/NIOSH manual. The head of the committee should report directly to the health and safety program director. The committee should meet regularly and during working hours. Attendance should be mandatory, meetings should be open to all employees and administrators, and minutes should be available to all theater personnel.

Here are some of the most important tasks for theater and shop HSCs.

Evaluation of materials and processes. The HSC should request and keep on file Material Safety Data Sheets and other hazard and ingredient information for all products used in the theater or shop. Ideally, this ingredient and hazard information should be obtained for products before they are purchased so that an item's safety can be ascertained before it is used. The committee should evaluate materials, choose the safest products, and educate personnel about how to work safely with them. Personnel should not be allowed to bring their own chemicals and materials to work without committee investigation and approval. Taking these steps also makes it possible to comply with most states' right-to-know laws and regulations.

The HSC also should investigate equipment before purchase, and it should make recommendations about safety.

Personal protective equipment selection. The HSC should investigate gloves, goggles, respirators, and other kinds of personal protective equipment and make recommendations about purchases. Although the employer actually is the party responsible for developing a written respiratory protection program (as required by OSHA if respirators are used more than very occasionally), the HSC may give advice.

Establishing information resources. A small collection of health and safety texts and catalogs should be available to all personnel and to HSC members to help them interpret Material Safety Data Sheets, evaluate products, and so on. Some of the publications listed in the bibliography would make appropriate selections. In addition, a network of advisors and experts from other theaters, schools, libraries, and governmental organizations should be developed so you can call them for advice.

Training and education. Accidents and health hazards can be avoided in any setting, no matter how dangerous, when people are formally trained about the hazards, and when the right methods of controlling the hazards are applied. Everyone knows—especially the experts—that where there are stairs, people will trip; where there are machine tools and saws, people will cut themselves; and where there are scaffolds, people will fall. However, *how many* people will trip, cut themselves, or fall will depend on how well trained and informed they are and how well secured, guarded, maintained, and protected the hazardous areas or equipment are.

Planning and training of personnel, teachers, and students should involve HSC participation. Training should consist of general orientation sessions for everyone (and should be repeated for all newly hired personnel or for new students) and special sessions should be held whenever a new process or material is added.

General orientation should include a fire safety session during which each person briefly discharges each type of fire extinguisher in the facility. Such training is necessary because each type of extinguisher operates differently. Once a fire starts, it is too late to read directions.

In colleges and universities, students should be required to take health and safety courses as part of their academic training programs. Such courses should include instruction in hazards and precautions, information about OSHA, Worker's Compensation, and the many federal, state, and local codes and laws that will regulate their work and protect their lives when they begin working.

Rulemaking. Setting up and enforcing safety rules should be part of the committee's work. Unfortunately, only rules will encourage some employees to work safely.

Accident/illness reporting and investigation. Theaters and shops should record and investigate all accidents, work-related illnesses, and incidents (accidents narrowly avoided). Such records are necessary to help stop the same things from happening in the future. The HSC should participate in investigating and evaluating these reports. (You may use OSHA accident and illness reporting forms.)

Emergency procedures. Written plans for emergencies and evacuation of the premises should be prepared with the help of fire marshals and other experts. The HSC should participate in writing and evaluating these plans. Scene and prop shops should consider plans for dealing with fires and serious accidents. Evacuation of large theaters is more complex, so various fire, police, and medical services must be consulted; specialists in developing written evacuation plans may be employed.

How to remove a disabled theater patron in an emergency is of special importance and requires planning. Two trained people will be needed if a patron in a wheelchair must be carried. Patrons whose life-support system is in their wheelchair should not be seated in an area from which they must be carried during an evacuation. Individuals who are blind or hearing-impaired may need only one person's assistance.

Considering these problems, safety dictates that the number of disabled in a theater at any one time should be limited by the number of staff members who are capable of protecting and assisting them in an emergency. Certainly any project such as a special performance for large numbers of the disabled should be discouraged unless extensive protective measures have been taken. Imagine if a theater fire were combined with aisles blocked by wheelchairs and numbers of people who had to move slowly or were unable to hear or understand commands! Give the same kinds of considerations to disabled students in schools as well.

Inspection and checklist development. Theaters and shops should be inspected both daily and periodically to check for different things. Daily inspections might include, for example, seeing that housekeeping and sanitation procedures are being carried out and that electrical equipment and machinery are working properly. Periodic inspections, on the other hand, might be monthly or bimonthly. They would detect changes in operation and equipment, for example, checking on ventilation rates of local exhaust equipment, restocking first aid kits, and arranging preventive maintenance checks on machinery.

Use a checklist when you inspect. Just as a shopping list keeps you from forgetting items at the market, safety checklists ensure complete inspections.

Developing a complete inspection list takes much thought and planning. Using preexisting checklists developed for similar facilities as a guideline or consulting outside experts may be helpful. But be aware that your own familiarity with a facility may hamper your ability to see hazards because you are simply too accustomed to their presence. You also should develop temporary checklists for individual theatrical productions to check props, lighting, and rigging, both during rehearsals and the run.

The HSC should help develop all types of inspection checklists and evaluate inspection reports.

Security. Securing your theater or workshop against theft, vandalism, intrusion of unauthorized people takes careful planning. If yours is a large facility, you will need security experts and trained staff. For small theaters and shops, the HSC may aid the administration in planning and executing security measures. Advice from local police and other experts should be sought and evaluated by HSC members. Be sure to develop rules, procedures, and security checklists.

Rules restricting access to keys and off-hour work are particularly important in reducing security breaches in small facilities. Minors and high school theater students, for example, *never* should be given keys to the theater or shops, nor should they be permitted to work unsupervised. Students cannot be expected to protect school property from theft or vandalism. Should either occur, the students with the keys usually will find themselves suspected of the crime. Should an accident occur under these circumstances, or should the student be assaulted or harmed by an intruder, the teacher may be liable.

There are many other things an HSC will consider. These will vary according to the needs of a particular theater or shop. In any case, the HSC is crucial to theater safety because every group needs an organization-wide effort to coordinate its program. One person or one union, no matter how powerful, cannot make theaters and shops safe. And even an HSC cannot do the job without the support of the administration. Theater safety requires efforts from everyone involved.

Safety hazards

Rigging safety

Attaching scenery to stage rigging systems and operating them are the most hazardous parts of theater production. Stage rigging systems include: hemp rope-sandbag balance systems; counter-weight systems using hemp and wire ropes; dead-hung or nonmovable rigging; and the newer remote-control electrical winch systems. Discussing all the hazards and precautions for each of these systems is beyond the scope of this book, but others that treat the subject in detail are in the bibliography. You can also consult instructional literature of the construction and maritime-rigging industries because their techniques are applicable to theater.

Some general recommendations, however, can be made to improve rigging safety procedures.

Arrange work schedules so that you *undertake rigging and flying when no other activities are taking place* on stage.

Permit only authorized and trained personnel to rig scenery and operate rigging systems. Make sure that rigging trainees or students have completed prerequisite courses in stagecraft and rigging, have stage experience, and are closely supervised.

Hold a *safety and strategy meeting* at the beginning of each work period for the entire crew. If students or trainees are present, review safety procedures and warning-call terminology.

Define each individual's job. Everyone should know precisely what his or her responsibilities are as defined the *Handbook of Theatrical Apprentices* or a job description.

Establish lines of command firmly. For example, the crew head or technical director should be the only one who calls instructions to the grid crew.

Order and *insist upon periods of complete silence* on stage during especially hazardous operations, such as when an arbor is being loaded or unloaded. Never allow noise to reach levels that could cover warning-calls.

Empty all pockets before going onto the grid. Crew members should make sure that nothing on their person—glasses, jewelry, hair ornaments—could fall to the stage. Secure all tools to workers with safety lines.

Wear safety belts while working on the grid.

Wear protective clothing appropriate to the type of work. Wear hard hats whenever overhead rigging is in process, and wear rubber-soled shoes or boots at all times.

Never drop anything from the grid to the floor. Ropes and electrical lines must be pulled up, coiled, and carried or lowered to stage level.

Check rigging and have it approved when it is finished. In a school, it may be approved by a faculty supervisor or an outside private inspector. Since faulty rigging can cause such serious accidents, paying a private inspector's fee (usually between $500 and $1,000) is often worthwhile, helping both to avoid accidents and protect liability.

Report any defective or worn equipment immediately and seek replacements.

Do not use equipment whose load-bearing capacity is not known—such as cardboard or drapes.

Report any accidents, incidents, or foreseeable problems immediately.

Once rigging is in place and being used, *report and discuss any problems* during rehearsal notes.

Strike show rigging—including extraneous hardware, batten extensions, and other attachments—at the end of each production's run.

Lighting and electrical safety

Lighting teachers, theater technicians, and students need solid knowledge of the principles of electricity and of electrical standards and codes.

Codes. Either the National Electrical Code (NEC) or the *NEC Handbook,* which annotates and explains the code, should be a basic reference for lighting designers and technicians. The code can be obtained from the National Fire Protection Association (NFPA) and updated editions are available every three years.

Since US municipalities commonly adopt the NEC as their local code, theater lighting workers familiar with the NEC will often be prepared to meet code requirements without further instruction. Some communities—New York City and Chicago, for example—have their own codes that sometimes are stricter. Lighting technicians should check routinely with local authorities to obtain up-to-date information on local codes.

The NFPA also publishes building and fire codes. Schools, libraries, and theater technicians should have copies of these codes and any additional local codes. You can obtain local codes from local building departments or fire marshals.

Electricity. Much is required to achieve electrical safety. Some of these important safety elements are ignored in small show houses and school theaters.

Ground all tools. All fixed wiring (conduited wiring terminating in outlets, light fixtures, for example) and temporary wiring (lighting systems, flexible cable, for example) should be three-wired. Three-wiring means that you can ground every tool and piece of equipment. Old theaters or school theaters with two-wire systems should be rewired or not used.

Use UL approved equipment. Every light, tool, or piece of equipment should be UL (Underwriters Laboratory) listed.

Discard old asbestos-coated wires (K wires).

All dimmers and light boards should have a dead (non-conducting) front.

Equip outlets with ground fault interrupters (GFIs) to provide back-up protection against shocks.

Use only three-wire heavy duty (number 16 or lower) extension cords. Never use zip cord (number 18 wire) or other light duty cords.

Protect temporary wiring, such as loose cords and flexible cable, from traffic. For example, cover a wire across a walkway with a treadle.

Theatrical lighting. By definition, theatrical lighting is temporary. All code provisions for temporary wiring apply to theater lighting, but here are some especially important general recommendations.

No other activities should take place on stage while lights are being hung or focused, so arrange work schedules accordingly.

Permit only authorized and trained personnel to work on lighting. Training should include basic first aid and emergency treatment for shock victims. Lighting trainees and students should be required to complete courses on stagecraft and lighting, should have stage experience, and should be supervised closely.

Never work alone on hazardous lighting procedures, such as hooking up panels. Organize "buddy system" work schedules.

Hold a safety and strategy meeting at the beginning of each work period for the entire crew. If students or trainees are present, review safety procedures. For example, be sure new students know the location of the master switch for stage lighting equipment.

Define each individual's job. Everyone should know precisely what his or her responsibilities are as defined by the *Handbook of Theatrical Apprentices* or a job description.

Establish lines of command and discipline firmly.

Empty all pockets before hanging lights. Crew members should make sure that nothing on their person—glasses, jewelry, hair ornaments— could fall to the stage. Secure all tools to workers with safety lines.

Wear protective clothing appropriate to the work. You might, for example, wear rubber-soled shoes and heat-resistant gloves. Wear hard hats when overhead hazards are present.

Report irregularities, defective equipment, or incidence of electrical shock, no matter how slight, immediately.

Know your instruments. Read lighting equipment directions and product information carefully. For example, a quartz lamp can explode if you touch it at any time with your bare hands.

Never overload dimmer boards.

Coil cables and cords neatly to avoid safety hazards, heat buildup, and magnetic field interference.

Have lighting inspected and approved by a licensed electrician.

Ladders

Work with lighting and rigging often requires use of ladders, but many theater technicians are unaware that many federal and local codes regulate ladder use. Familiarize yourself with rules about ladders in the General Industry Standards and with local codes that may apply. Some commonsense rules about the use of ladders include:

Inspect ladders before use.

Never substitute a chair or box for a small ladder.

Install non-skid feet on any straight ladder. Tie off ladders, block them, or have an assistant support them against slipping when you use them.

Use straight ladders only on clean, level surfaces. Lean them against a surface at a distance of approximately one-quarter of the length of the ladder. Never lean ladders against free-hanging pipes or other unstable surfaces.

Use stepladders only in completely open positions. Use only the side with steps for climbing or support. Never stand on the top step.

Never leave tools on a ladder, and never drop or pitch tools to another worker.

Use wooden ladders, if possible, because they are non-conducting, heavier, and usually stabler.

Make sure at least two people assist at the base of *large A-frame ladders* with extensions to secure them against tipping.

Rather than carrying heavy objects up a ladder, it is safer to climb a ladder, drop a line, and *haul the object up.*

Irregular surfaces

Take some special precautions to work safely when walking surfaces are uneven or raked. Accidents easily occur near stairs, pits, traps, or other changes in elevation.

Discuss hazards formally with all performers and personnel prior to any work or rehearsals involving the hazard.

Inform all performers and personnel of designated "safe routes" where traffic will be routed to avoid the hazard. No one should be allowed to approach hazardous changes in elevation unless absolutely necessary.

Mark changes in elevation on the stage with phosphorescent tape so that they are more easily seen in the dark.

Mark pits, traps, and other hazards with large signs, and barricade them when they are not in use. Mark open pits and traps with a ghost light (standing lamp) when they are not in use.

Give performers extra rehearsal time to learn to work safely with elevation changes.

Obtain variances from OSHA for hazardous changes in walking surface elevation.

Other safety hazards

A vast variety of other hazards exists in theaters: scaffolds, revolving platforms, and elevators are just a few. It is incumbent on theater administrators or teachers to research hazards and safety precautions and to make sure that all federal and local codes and standards are being met.

The strike

Strikes should receive special attention because they combine all the previously mentioned hazardous activities with their own dangers. Lighting, rigging, and electrical safety precautions are especially important during strikes. Disipline and planning should replace hurried activity. Common sense is prerequisite for all participants. A strike is not a time for a party. Do not hurry a strike in order to get to a party.

Many high school and college theater teachers report more accidents and injuries during strikes than during other phases of production. Teachers must be especially careful to maintain discipline. Without discipline, latent destructive urges of a student—especially an adolescent student—can quickly transform dissassembly into demolition.

Health hazards

Theater health hazards are complicated to understand because theater workers use so many different materials, and bodily responses vary greatly.

Hazardous materials used in theater

At one time or another, practically all types of consumer products and many industrial ones have been used in theater to achieve just the right look or effect. Fortunately, information about the hazards of the *chemical ingredients* in these products can be found in medical and occupational health literature: techniques that protect industrial workers can also protect theater workers.

Precautions similar to those used in industry are also needed for the *industrial processes* used in theater. Theater workers breathe in the same gases and fumes when they weld; they inhale the same solvents and pigments as painters, the same wood dusts and glues as woodworkers, and so on. So theater workers need to be well informed about the hazards of the processes they use. Here are some basic occupational/health concepts about toxic materials and hazardous processes.

Acute effects, by definition, are sharp and severe, occur suddenly, and run a short course. This short course can end in complete recovery, recovery with some disability, or—at worst—death. Acute occupational illnesses are brought about by a massive exposure to a toxic material. Such illnesses usually are easy to diagnose because their causes and effects are easily linked. For example, exposure to solvents such as lacquer thinner or turpentine can cause effects ranging from mild narcosis (lightheadedness) to more severe narcosis (headache, nausea, loss of coordination) to unconsciousness and death, depending on the severity of the exposure.

If the exposure to the solvent stops soon enough, complete recovery can be expected. If the exposure is much greater, permanent brain damage (including epileptic-like seizures), liver damage, or kidney damage may result. Whatever the effects, the symptoms usually begin to express themselves during or shortly after the exposure, making their cause obvious.

Chronic effects are much harder to diagnose. They may last for life and are caused by repeated exposure to low doses of toxic materials, usually over a long period of time. Symptoms may vary from person to person, and, because they appear very gradually, they are commonly attributed to causes other than the toxic exposure.

For example, consider lacquer thinner or turpentine solvents. In large amounts they will produce acute effects. But regular exposure at lower doses over a period of months or years might produce individualized chronic effects like dermatitis (if skin contact is involved), psychological problems (apathy, irritability, depression), or chronic liver, kidney, and nervous-system damage.

Cancer. Occupational cancers are a special type of chronic illness caused by cancer-causing agents, *carcinogens.* Unlike ordinary toxic substances whose effects vary with dose, evidence suggests that there is no safe level of exposure to carcinogens. Theoretically one molecule of a carcinogen in the right place at the right time can cause cancer. However, the greater the dose, the greater the risk that cancer will occur.

Once exposed to a carcinogen, the person exposed typically experiences the onset of symptoms ten to forty years later. By this time people may have forgotten what chemicals they used; even if they remember, the connection between the chemical and the cancer is almost impossible to prove.

Some people are fatalistic about exposure to carcinogens because they believe that "everything causes cancer." They cite the almost constant flow of news stories about dioxin, PCBs (transformer fluid), asbestos, and the like. This flood of new cancer information has been happening in recent decades because for many years most substances were not tested for their cancer-causing potential before they entered the marketplace. It is estimated that each year between 1,500 and 3,000 new chemicals even now enter the workplace similarly untested. Recent testing programs are turning up more than a few carcinogens among them, although some experts estimate that less than one percent of workplace chemicals cause cancer.

Other people are careless about exposure to carcinogens because they mistrust the animal tests used to identify carcinogens. These people reason that overdoses of any chemical, even water, will kill animals. This is true, but only chemicals with the unique ability to participate in altering a cell's genetic material can cause cancer.

Chemicals that cause cancer in animals are considered "suspect carcinogens." Proven "human carcinogens," on the other hand, are substances associated with statistically significant numbers of cancer cases in studies of large numbers of people who are exposed to the substance. Experience has shown that suspect carcinogens can almost always be reclassified as human carcinogens as soon as a large enough exposed population is identified. Prudence dictates considering both categories of carcinogens hazardous.

Two examples of the many suspect carcinogens used in theater are formaldehyde (from plywood, and urea formaldehyde foams and adhesives), and cleaning solvents such as trichloroethylene. Some human carcinogens found in theater are dyes chemically derived from benzidine, asbestos, and wood dust.

Sensitizers. Anyone who has reacted badly to poison ivy has experienced a strong sensitizer. A sensitizer is simply a chemical that can provoke an allergic response in significant numbers of people.

Many of the chemicals used in theater crafts are strong sensitizers. Epoxy resins and their curing agents, for example, have been shown through industrial studies to arouse allergies (usually in the form of dermatitis or asthma) in more than 50 percent of the workers who use them.

Other such substances include turpentine, the isocyanates (in urethane casting and foaming chemicals), chrome compounds (found in some cosmetics), nickel (in some welding fumes), formaldehyde, fiber-reactive dyes, California redwood and other woods, and many more.

People often consider allergies a minor health problem, but they are not. The presence of an allergy signifies an immune system error or overreaction. Once this overreaction develops, the individual then may react allergically to all chemically similar substances. He or she may be more likely to develop additional allergies, ones that will last a lifetime or tend to increase in severity with continued exposure.

Allergies disable many industrial workers yearly and cause many others to leave their jobs. Obviously allergy merits serious concern, yet in theater the victim is often blamed and thought of as a complainer or somehow unfit. Instead, materials containing strong sensitizers should be identified and exposure avoided.

How toxic materials enter the body

In order to cause damage, toxic materials must enter the body. Entry can occur in three ways: through skin contact, inhalation, and ingestion.

Skin contact. The skin's barrier of waxes, oils, and dead cells can be destroyed by chemicals like acids, caustics, solvents, peroxides, and bleaches. Once the skin's defenses are breached, some of these chemicals can damage the skin itself, the tissues beneath the skin, or even enter the blood where they can be transported throughout the body causing damage to other organs.

Cuts, abrasions, burns, rashes, and other violations of the skin's barrier also can allow chemicals to penetrate into the blood and be transported throughout the body. There are also many chemicals that can—without your knowing it—enter the blood through undamaged skin. Among these are toluene, benzene, xylene, phenol, and methyl alcohol.

Inhalation. Many inhaled substances can acutely damage the respiratory system from nose and sinuses to lungs. The damage they may cause ranges from minor irritation of the respiratory tract to nose bleeds and life-threatening chemical pneumonia, depending on how irritating the substance is and how much is inhaled. Small doses of irritants inhaled repeatedly over years can cause chronic respiratory damage, such as chronic bronchitis or emphysema.

Examples of substances that can cause chronic and acute respiratory irritation and damage include welding fumes, fumes from heating or burning plastics, cigarette smoke, and many chemical dusts.

Some substances also pass through lung tissue, enter the blood, and damage other organs. Examples of some of these illnesses include kidney damage from turpentine, kidney and nervous-system damage from lead-containing spray paints, and liver damage and cancer from some dry cleaning solvents.

Ingestion. You can accidentally ingest toxic materials by eating, smoking, or drinking while working, or by touching soiled hands to your mouth, biting your nails, or from similar habits. The lung's mucous also traps dusts: you inhale them, cough them up, and then swallow them.

Every year some accidental ingestions occur when chemicals are poured into glasses or paper cups and people later mistake them for beverages. Some of these accidents have seriously harmed children who were allowed into the workplace or home studio. Be sure to keep theater materials out of children's reach.

Are you at risk?

It seems there are always toxic materials in theater work. But how serious is the exposure? At what point should you become concerned? To help you (and your doctor) find out if the exposure is significant, you should be able to answer the following questions about each of the materials you use.

How much do you use?. Keep track of the amounts of materials you use. Obviously, a gallon of a substance is potentially more hazardous than a pint.

Under what conditions are you exposed? Does your workplace have good ventilation and protective equipment, or are you working in a small unvented room, breathing the vapors, getting it on your hands, and so on?

How often are you exposed? Do you use the material every day, twice a week, or once a month? Do you use it two hours a day, eight hours a day, or longer? Since theater workers may have varied work schedules, you may need to keep a work diary to answer this question completely. (There are also OSHA standards for how much exposure employees may be expected to endure.)

How toxic are the materials you use? Some materials are much more toxic than others. Learn which materials you use are the most hazardous. Keep Material Safety Data Sheets on file.

What are your "total body burdens" of toxic substances? Your total body burden of a substance is the total amount of that substance in your body from all possible sources. For instance, if you work with lead-pigmented scene paints, your body burden of lead would be the sum of the lead you absorb on the job, plus the lead from the air you breathe (especially if you live in a city), and the lead in your food and water. You also have body burdens of cadmium, carbon monoxide, pesticides, and many other substances. Body burdens influence each other: for example, alcoholic beverage consumption adds to the effects of solvent exposure.

Are you a member of a high-risk group? Some people are physiologically much more susceptible then most to the harmful effects of chemicals. Among these are smokers, drinkers, children, the elderly, people with chronic diseases or allergies, and people taking certain kinds of medications. At especially high risk is the pregnant woman and her baby. All of these groups should be especially vigilant in avoiding workplace chemical exposures.

Exposure standards

If you suspect that your workplace air contains health-threatening amounts of a substance, you may need to know how these amounts can be measured. There are two sets of exposure standards for airborne concentrations of many solvent vapors, dusts, metal fumes, and other substances.

Threshold Limit Values (TLVs). Time-weighted average TLVs are set by the American Conference of Governmental Industrial Hygienists (ACGIH) which defines them as "airborne concentrations of substances and conditions under which it is believed that nearly all workers may be repeatedly exposed day after day without adverse effect."

The TLVs are usually expressed in milligrams per cubic meter of air (mg/m^3) or in parts per million of air (ppm). Detecting the exact concentration of substances in air requires the use of special air-sampling equipment or devices. You can retain industrial hygienists to sample air.

Even if the air concentrations do not exceed the TLV, be aware (1) that some workers may be affected by lower-than-TLV levels of air contaminants; (2) that workers—healthy adults—are being considered, not children, the aged, the sick, or other high-risk groups; and (3) that day-after-day exposure means eight-hour work days, not long hours of overtime or work at home where twenty-four-hour-a-day exposures can result.

Permissible Exposure Limits (PELs). OSHA, a federal agency with legal powers to set and enforce standards, establishes PELs. PELs, for the most part, are based on the 1968 TLVs with some changes for particular chemicals. TLVs are revised yearly and generally provide more protection for workers than the PELs. However, the ACGIH is just an advisory group of professionals and the organization's standards are merely recommendations; OSHA standards are the law.

There are also TLVs and PELs for physical hazards such as heat, radiation (laser, ultraviolet, etc.), and noise. The intent of these standards is to keep work-place hazards below levels that can cause harm or occupational illnesses.

Occupational illnesses and their causes

Here are some of the diseases associated with chemicals or other hazards found in theater work.

Skin diseases. Various types of dermatitis, a general term meaning inflammation of the skin, can result from skin contact with harsh soaps, acids, solvents, and other chemicals. For example, washing the hands with a solvent such as turpentine can cause a number of skin effects including drying, reddening, chapping, driving other contaminants deeper into the skin, and allergic reactions.

Allergic dermatitis is a common industrial illness. In many instances, allergic dermatitis spreads to other parts of the body. On rare occasions, skin all over a person's body becomes affected and the disease can be life-threatening. Several such cases have been known among workers exposed to epoxy.

The chemicals in some cosmetics also are known to cause allergic dermatitis. In addition some cosmetics can cause acne and may exacerbate *infections.*

Skin cancer may be caused by exposure to ultraviolet light from welding, carbon arc lights, and the like, and from exposure to chemicals such as arsenic and lampblack.

Eye diseases. Many theater materials can damage eyes or even lead to *blindness.* Dusts and particles from metal grindings, glitter dust, and fiberglass, and other materials can injure and irritate eyes. Ultraviolet light can damage the eye's cornea to cause *arc eye* or can damage the lens to create a type of *cataract.*

Splashes of solvents, ammonia, acids, or peroxides can damage the eyes se-verely. Theater workers who are lax about wearing eye protection should be re-minded that one splash of a liquid such as the peroxides used to cure polyester resins has caused permanent blindness.

Contact lenses can exacerbate damage to eyes exposed to dusts, solvent vap-ors, splashes, and the like. *Conjunctivitis* and eye *infections* are common complica-tions of eye cosmetics.

Respiratory system diseases. The respiratory system is composed of the upper respiratory tract (nose, sinuses, throat, and larynx) and the lower respiratory tract (the lungs). This system contains mucous membranes and delicate lung tissues that are especially susceptible to airborne contaminants.

Any irritating dust, vapor, fume, or mist can be potentially hazardous to the respiratory system. For example, low doses of moderately irritating substances (such as small amounts of ammonia and formaldehyde released by acrylic paints) may result in slight damage to respiratory tissues that may leave workers more vulnerable to *colds* and *infections*.

Heavier exposures to more highly irritating substances (such as solvents or oil mists) can lead to diseases such as *acute bronchitis* or *chemical pneumonia*. Theater workers should be aware that colds, bronchitis, and pneumonia that are attributed to infectious agents may have started from a chemical exposure.

Years of exposure to airborne substances can lead to chronic respiratory diseases such as *chronic bronchitis* and *emphysema*. Theater welders also may be at risk from *lung scarring* (pulmonary fibrosis). Respiratory system *cancers* also can be caused by a number of substances found in theater work, including asbestos, cadmium, some welding fumes, and wood dust.

Smokers are at greater risk from lung cancer and almost all of the other diseases of the lungs. Smoking inhibits the lungs' natural clearing mechanisms, leaving toxic dusts and particles in them longer and allowing them to do more damage.

Airborne substances may cause allergic responses ranging from *hay fever-like symptoms* and *asthma* to *hypersensitivity pneumonia*. Substances known to cause serious allergic responses include fiber-reactive dyes, some wood dusts, urethane casting and foaming chemicals, and formaldehyde.

Heart and blood diseases. Many solvents at high doses can alter the heart's rhythm (*arrhythmia*), and even cause a *heart attack*. Deaths related to this phenomenon have been noted among both industrial workers and glue-sniffers whose levels of exposure to solvents were very high.

Benzene, still found as a contaminant in some solvents, can cause *aplastic anemia* and *leukemia*.

Physical and mental stress also are known to affect the heart and circulatory system. Since unreasonable deadlines seem to be the rule rather than the exception in theater, these health effects on the heart are another good reason to alter the routine urgent deadline pattern in theater.

Nervous system diseases. Metals like lead and mercury are known to cause *nervous system damage*. Symptoms may be irritability, psychological problems, decreased mental acuity, or loss of coordination. The psychological problems may be characterized by depression, memory loss, confusion, and explosive anger. They are well depicted by the traits of the Mad Hatter in Lewis Carroll's *Alice in Wonderland*, a stereotype of mid-nineteenth-century hatters who worked with mercury-treated felt.

Theater workers may be exposed to lead during soldering, during welding of metals coated with lead paint or alloyed with lead, or while using lead pigments like molybdate (moly) orange or chrome yellow.

Almost all solvents can affect the nervous system similarly. Symptoms vary from mild *narcosis* (lightheadedness, headache, dizziness) to *coma* and *death* at high doses. People exposed to small amounts of solvent daily for years often exhibit the symptoms of *chronic nervous system damage* such as memory loss, mental confusion, sleep disturbances, and depression.

Normal hexane (n-hexane) is particularly damaging to the nervous system and chronic exposure to it can cause *toxic neuropathy*, a disease similar to multiple sclerosis. N-hexane is commonly found in spray adhesives, rubber cement, and rubber cement thinner.

Other organ-system diseases. Liver damage or hepatitis is usually thought of as a viral disease, but it can be caused by some toxic metals and most solvents (even grain alcohol, the least toxic of all solvents) if doses are high enough.

Carbon tetrachloride, still used as a spot remover or cleaner by some theater workers, can cause severe liver damage and *liver cancer*. It is banned in consumer products because it also works synergistically with alcohol. People have died because they drank an alcoholic beverage while working with this solvent.

Kidney damage also is caused by many solvents and metals. Turpentine, chlorinated cleaning solvents (like trichloroethylene), and lead are particularly hazardous to the kidneys. Red blood cells and muscle tissue can be damaged by electrical shock or severe accidents, causing debris to block the kidneys' tiny tubules.

Bladder cancer is associated with dyes and pigments derived from the chemical benzidine. In the past, ordinary household and union dyes commonly contained these dyes, and some still may contain them.

Miscarriages, birth defects, sterility, loss of sex drive. All of these have come to be associated with chemical and radiation exposures. Both men and women's reproductive systems can be affected.

Certain chemicals in epoxy resins (the diglycidal ethers) and the cellosolves (chemicals also called glycol ethers found in some paints and spray cleaners) atrophy testicles and cause birth defects in animals. Lead and many solvents can lower sex drive in both men and women and some studies of humans have associated them with birth defects and miscarriages.

During pregnancy, women are more vulnerable to many toxic substances. Even more vulnerable is the fetus. Solvents (including alcohol) and many metals should be avoided during pregnancy. The fetus is most at risk in the earliest weeks, before the woman knows she is pregnant, so women should plan to avoid toxic chemical exposures when trying to conceive. Vigilance against exposure to toxic substances should continue through breast feeding, since many chemicals can be ingested by infants through mother's milk. For more information, see the Center for Occupational Hazards' data sheet, "Reproductive Hazards in the Arts and Crafts."

Children and toxic materials

People who teach theater crafts to children, parents of children who work in theater, or theater craftspeople who work at home or with children around them should be very aware that children are far more susceptible to toxic materials than adults.

Children's rapid metabolisms permit more substances to be incorporated and absorbed by their bodies; their brains and nervous systems are still developing and are particularly susceptible. Very young children also have incompletely developed lung and body defenses. Body weight is a factor, too: the smaller the child, the greater the risk from toxic materials.

Children under twelve are also at risk for psychological reasons. At this age they cannot be expected to understand the hazards of materials, nor can they be expected to carry out precautionary procedures effectively or consistently. Adults who expose children to toxic materials in classes or during theatrical productions may find themselves liable for injuries or illnesses. In particular, children under twelve should not be exposed to any solvent, solvent-containing material, toxic metals, powdered dyes or pigments, aerosol sprays, photographic chemicals, epoxy resins, or dusts. Many safe paints, papier-mâché preparations, glues, and the like are on the market. The Center for Occupational Hazards' data sheet "Children's Art Supplies Can Be Toxic" lists safe products.

II

What you can do

Sources of information

Developing health and safety programs and cooperating with already-established ones are obviously the best means of protection. Realistically, however, many theater craftspeople find themselves alone in situations where they must find immediate solutions and make quick decisions. This section contains facts about product labels that every theater worker should know. These facts will help you make informed choices.

Consumer product labels

People tend to assume—because a product is sold by a reputable distributor and has a label—that someone has investigated the hazards of all the ingredients. The truth is that some ingredients in both consumer and industrial products never have been tested for acute hazards, and many have never been tested for chronic hazards (such as cancer). Manufacturers and even some regulatory agencies tend to consider chemicals innocent until proven guilty; because literally thousands of new chemicals enter the marketplace yearly, the docket is too crowded to bring more than a handful to trial.

This basic problem aside, there are some general standards for labels. Labels should indicate clearly (1) what the product is; (2) the manufacturer's name and address; (3) directions for use; and (4) acute hazard and precaution information. In addition, some products contain ingredients for which special labeling requirements exist. For example, labels on products that can harm plumbing or pollute water supplies must have printed advice about how to dispose of them properly.

Most theater product labeling deficiencies occur because many manufacturers and distributors of theatrical products are small businesses that have developed with a minimum of governmental scrutiny. No one has demanded that they pay attention to complex labeling requirements.

Theatrical supply outlets are almost the only place in the American business community selling *unlabeled products*; hazardous dyes and pigments still are scooped from bins into paper sacks and sold without proper identification. Other products such as fog-making liquids, fire retardants, and plastic resin products also are purchased by distributors in bulk and resold to customers in unlabeled containers. Such products invite accidental misuse.

Many theatrical products are *improperly labeled*; they fail to include vital information such as the manufacturer's address or precautions about use. Theater workers should read labels carefully, and they should reject products with deficient labels or ask their manufacturers to provide the missing information.

Some companies' labels not only meet standards but also exceed them. They go so far as to *provide additional information* such as lists and amounts of ingredients—information needed not only to protect health but also to allow the quality of work to be controlled for uniformity. Theater workers should choose these well labeled products whenever possible.

Label terminology. Phrases and words on labels often have strict legal definitions and can mislead if people assume the words mean something else. Some widely misunderstood terms include the following.

Many people believe that *"use with adequate ventilation"* means you should work with a window open. It really means you need to provide sufficient ventilation to keep airborne concentrations of a product's mist, dust, fume, or vapor below the levels considered hazardous for the user. In the case of an adult employee, this would mean that airborne levels should be kept below the TLV.

Conditions that can provide this safe level could vary from working in a very large space (when using very small amounts of moderately toxic materials), to working in a spray booth or with some other local exhaust system (when using larger amounts or more toxic materials).

You must know certain facts in order to plan such ventilation. For example, to calculate ventilation air-flow rates, you must know exactly what substance a product gives off or releases. Ironically, this is often precisely the information the manufacturer withholds. Theater workers should demand ingredient information for products whose labels indicate a need for ventilation.

The words *"poison," "danger," "warning," or "caution"* on a label indicate the presence of a toxic substance or mixture. Usually these labels reflect the results of biological testing required by the Federal Hazardous Substances Act (FHSA) in the United States and in the Hazardous Products Act (HPA) in Canada. (Cosmetics are labeled in accordance with the Food, Drug and Cosmetics Act and presumably would contain no substances requiring such labeling.) These tests involve single dose, *acute* exposures of animals by means of skin contact, eye contact, inhalation, and ingestion. The Center for Occupational Hazards has found that some small manufacturers of theatrical products are not aware that the FHSA requires these tests for consumer products.

The FHSA ingestion test, for example, consists of feeding ten rats an amount of the product (five grams per kilogram of body weight) and waiting two weeks. After this time has elapsed, if *half or more* of the rats are dead, the manufacturer must put a *"toxic"* warning label on the product.

The FHSA also regulates nontoxic labeling. In the ingestion test, for example, if *fewer than half* the rats die, the product can be labeled *"nontoxic."* The distinction between toxic and nontoxic, therefore, is not as great as the average consumer would assume.

More importantly, these tests do not identify chemicals that cause *chronic* hazards—cancer, allergies, chronic poisoning (requiring more than a single dose), reproductive system damage, or birth defects. Using these tests as a standard, asbestos could carry a nontoxic label because it is incapable of killing rats in two weeks. (The effects of asbestos can take years to materialize.)

Some small companies put nontoxic labels on products without performing the FHSA tests. Some others legally label their products nontoxic, but promote injudicious product use by inspiring overconfidence. Theater workers should understand the very limited meaning of nontoxic and exercise due caution.

To avoid the more stringent governmental regulations for consumer product labeling, some theatrical product manufacturers label their products *"for professional use only"* or *"for industrial use only."* This exemption from consumer product labeling can easily mislead the unwary. Manufacturers and suppliers of these products are not supposed to make their products available to nonprofessional users such as individuals or public schools. Yet it is not unusual to see such products in just those places: in schools and in ordinary hardware and paint outlets. Catalog distributors also often make them available to any purchaser by mail.

Theater workers who use these products should always keep in mind that "for professional use only" labels are usually far less informative than consumer product labels. You should assume that such a product is safe to use only under strict professional or industrial conditions—not in small unvented or unequipped locations. Always obtain a Material Safety Data Sheet (MSDS) from the manufacturer prior to using such products (see page 35).

Labeling legislation. In response to the obvious inadequacies of current labeling laws, bills have been introduced at both the federal and state levels (in California, New York, Massachusetts, Illinois, Tennessee, New Jersey, Oregon, and Virginia) to improve the labeling of "art" materials. Other states are considering similar legislation.

These bills are of two different types. One type would provide chronic hazard labeling for all art materials, and the other would keep toxic art materials out of elementary schools. In California, Oregon, Illinois, and Tennessee, bills of both types have been signed into law and will take effect shortly. Selection of art materials used in theater arts classes in these states' elementary schools will probably be affected by the children's art materials bill. It remains to be seen whether the labeling of theater arts materials intended for older children and adults will be affected by the chronic hazards labeling bill. The results have not been tallied in other states.

Voluntary industry standards. For more than forty years, art materials manufacturers, through an industrial association, have set voluntary standards for children's art materials. The quality of the voluntary program has varied considerably over the years, but at present the Center for Occupational Hazards recommends products that meet these standards. Hundreds of materials including paints, chalks, modeling media, and water-based silk-screen products have been approved. Use these products with very young theater students; the products can be identified by labels that bear an AP (Approved Product) or CP (Certified Product) seal from the Arts and Crafts Materials Institute (ACMI). The Center for Occupational Hazards data sheet "Children's Art Supplies Can Be Toxic" provides further information on safe materials for young children.

Recently, the ACMI has begun certifying products that are appropriate for adults and children over twelve years of age. These products bear a CL (Certified Label) seal and their labels contain all the cautionary statements required by law plus the chronic hazard warnings necessary to meet a new standard developed through the American Society of Testing and Materials. Since this standard could be applied to most theater arts products as well, it may be that the remedy is already at hand for providing theater workers with products labeled adequately for chronic hazards.

A list of AP, CP, or CL products, or further information about how theater product manufacturers could comply with ACMI standards, can be obtained by writing to: The Arts and Crafts Materials Institute, Inc., 715 Boylston Street, Boston, MA 02116.

For additional information about labeling terminology, fire hazard warnings, and so on, read the Center for Occupational Hazards' data sheet, "Labels: Understanding and Using Them."

Rules for using label information

1. Do not purchase unlabeled or improperly labeled products.

2. Read labels carefully. Inadequate as many are, they are your first line of defense.

3. Request an MSDS and any additional product information you may need from the manufacturer, whose name and address should be on the label.

4. Exercise a purchasing bias in favor of products with good labels or CL seals, and whose manufacturers or distributors respond to requests for MSDSs and further information.

5. Follow up MSDS information by looking up information about ingredients or by consulting other experts. *Do not rely on antidote information without first checking with your local Poison Control Center.*

6. Do not rely heavily on the term "nontoxic."

7. Read and follow directions for use. Do not experiment unless experts agree that it will not be dangerous to use a product in a way not specified on the label.

8. Follow precautionary advice. For example, if a label warns about eye damage, wear goggles.

9. Demand complete information from manufacturers who label products "use with adequate ventilation" so you can plan for sufficient ventilation. Get manufacturers' recommendations for ventilation in writing, if possible.

10. Use products designated for professional or industrial use only in well-ventilated and well-equipped locations. Never use these products with children or untrained workers.

11. Use AP- or CP-seal products with children who are younger than twelve years old.

Fig. 1

Figure 1 Guide to the use of Material Safety Data Sheets

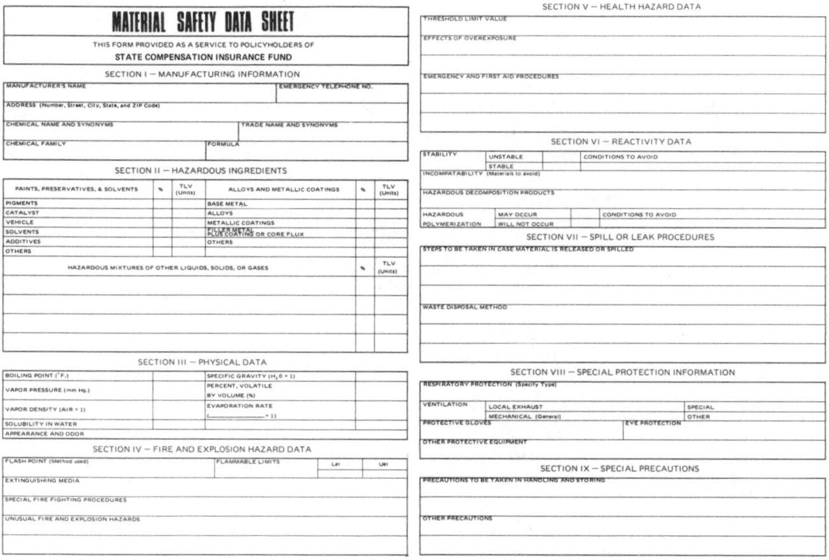

MATERIAL SAFETY DATA SHEET

THIS FORM PROVIDED AS A SERVICE TO POLICYHOLDERS OF
STATE COMPENSATION INSURANCE FUND

SECTION I — MANUFACTURING INFORMATION

MANUFACTURER'S NAME | EMERGENCY TELEPHONE NO.
ADDRESS (Number, Street, City, State, and ZIP Code)
CHEMICAL NAME AND SYNONYMS | TRADE NAME AND SYNONYMS
CHEMICAL FAMILY | FORMULA

SECTION II — HAZARDOUS INGREDIENTS

PAINTS, PRESERVATIVES, & SOLVENTS	%	TLV (Units)	ALLOYS AND METALLIC COATINGS	%	TLV (Units)
PIGMENTS			BASE METAL		
CATALYST			ALLOYS		
VEHICLE			METALLIC COATINGS		
SOLVENTS			FILLER METAL PLUS COATING OR CORE FLUX		
ADDITIVES			OTHERS		
OTHERS					

HAZARDOUS MIXTURES OF OTHER LIQUIDS, SOLIDS, OR GASES	%	TLV (Units)

SECTION III — PHYSICAL DATA

BOILING POINT (°F.)		SPECIFIC GRAVITY (H_2O = 1)	
VAPOR PRESSURE (mm Hg.)		PERCENT, VOLATILE BY VOLUME (%)	
VAPOR DENSITY (AIR = 1)		EVAPORATION RATE (________ = 1)	
SOLUBILITY IN WATER			
APPEARANCE AND ODOR			

SECTION IV — FIRE AND EXPLOSION HAZARD DATA

FLASH POINT (Method used) | FLAMMABLE LIMITS | Lel | Uel
EXTINGUISHING MEDIA
SPECIAL FIRE FIGHTING PROCEDURES
UNUSUAL FIRE AND EXPLOSION HAZARDS

SECTION V — HEALTH HAZARD DATA

THRESHOLD LIMIT VALUE
EFFECTS OF OVEREXPOSURE
EMERGENCY AND FIRST AID PROCEDURES

SECTION VI — REACTIVITY DATA

STABILITY | UNSTABLE | | CONDITIONS TO AVOID
| STABLE | |
INCOMPATABILITY (Materials to avoid)
HAZARDOUS DECOMPOSITION PRODUCTS
HAZARDOUS POLYMERIZATION | MAY OCCUR | | CONDITIONS TO AVOID
| WILL NOT OCCUR | |

SECTION VII — SPILL OR LEAK PROCEDURES

STEPS TO BE TAKEN IN CASE MATERIAL IS RELEASED OR SPILLED
WASTE DISPOSAL METHOD

SECTION VIII — SPECIAL PROTECTION INFORMATION

RESPIRATORY PROTECTION (Specify Type)
VENTILATION | LOCAL EXHAUST | SPECIAL
| MECHANICAL (General) | OTHER
PROTECTIVE GLOVES | EYE PROTECTION
OTHER PROTECTIVE EQUIPMENT

SECTION IX — SPECIAL PRECAUTIONS

PRECAUTIONS TO BE TAKEN IN HANDLING AND STORING
OTHER PRECAUTIONS

Source: MassCOSH Fact Sheet.

Material safety data sheets

Material Safety Data Sheets (MSDSs) are forms developed by OSHA and filled out by manufacturers. An MSDS provides such information as what ingredients are hazardous and what precautions to take. Theaters, shops, schools, and individual craftspeople should acquire MSDSs on all the products they use.

Who can request MSDSs? Anyone can request an MSDS, but in the past manufacturers were *not required* to make them available to customers. However, many responsible manufacturers have made it a practice to supply MSDSs as a courtesy.

During the last several years, about twenty states have passed "right-to-know" legislation giving many workers (including theater workers, in many states) the right to have MSDSs. There is now a federal law, the OSHA Hazards Communication Standard (effective November 1985), that requires all manufacturers, distributors, and importers to prepare MSDSs for their products and to make them available to many classes of industries. Included are shops or businesses producing: apparel and other textile products; lumber and wood products; printed and published materials; and fabricated metal products.

Theaters, schools, and individual consumers are not included on this list of industries in the federal OSHA Hazard Communication Standard. However, since suppliers should have them available for customers in these industries and for workers in right-to-know states, and since many responsible companies routinely provide them, it seems reasonable that schools, theaters, and individuals also should expect them upon request.

How to request MSDSs. Although anyone can request an MSDS from a manufacturer, employees subject to the federal and state right-to-know standards should ask their employers to obtain copies for them. The employer should write to the manufacturer, and an MSDS should be forthcoming.

Since schools, theaters, and shops use many different products, it is expedient to request MSDSs by means of a form letter on the institution's letterhead. Schools and other operations that place large orders often can get good results if they require an MSDS as part of their bid procedures. Such requirements give companies an economic incentive to provide MSDSs.

A simple letter might read "We request Material Safety Data Sheets on the following product(s)." More elaborate requests might refer to a particular state's right-to-know law, the institution's own health and safety program requirement, or any other pertinent reasons for the request.

The Center for Occupational Hazards suggests you keep copies of your MSDS correspondence. If manufacturers do not meet MSDS requests, send copies of your correspondence with the Center to them and an additional request will be sent on COH letterhead.

Evaluating MSDS Information. When you receive an answer to your request, be sure the form you have received is truly an MSDS. Some theatrical product manufacturers send special product information sheets and promotional material instead.

You also must evaluate MSDSs. Many MSDS forms contain errors or deliberately vague information. Others are models of clarity. Look for the following information in each MSDS section.

Section I identifies the product and its manufacturer. It also should list a telephone number at which further information can be obtained. Large companies may even have hotline numbers for emergencies. The section should further identify the product by chemical name, trade name, and chemical family. If there is no product identification, the section should include a statement that the material is "proprietary." Remember, using proprietary products means exposing workers to unknown chemicals.

Section II: Hazardous Ingredients should list all the ingredients for which OSHA has established standards, their Threshold Limit Values, and the percentage of each ingredient in the product. Remember, there are many hazardous ingredients for which no standards have been developed, so these ingredients probably will not be listed.

Section III: Physical Data includes information such as vapor pressure, boiling point, and the like, which can be used to help identify ingredients not properly listed in Section I and which can be useful in deciding how dangerous the product is.

Section IV: Fire and Explosion Data gives the flash point of the material—the temperature at which it will ignite in the presence of a flame or spark, the concentrations in air at which it could explode—and information about how to put out a fire involving the materials.

Section V: Health Hazard Data. Older MSDSs list only acute health hazard information here. Newer MSDSs also should list chronic effects as required by the OSHA Hazard Communication Standard, but you should not rely upon information in this section. Complete your investigation by referring to other sources.

Section VI: Reactivity Data tells about conditions that could cause the product to react dangerously or to decompose and release dangerous substances.

Section VII: Spill or Leak Procedures gives instructions about handling spills and disposing of spilled material.

Section VIII: Special Protection Information lists what protective equipment and type of ventilation to use with the material. Minimum measures are usually spelled out, and so you should seek additional sources of information when you plan purchases of protective equipment and ventilation.

Section IX: Special Precautions lists handling, storage, and other special safety measures.

Rules for using MSDSs

1. Request MSDSs on all products from manufacturers, distributors, or importers.

2. Do not use products (or phase out those already in use) for which MSDSs are not provided.

3. Evaluate MSDS information. If you need help evaluating MSDSs, send copies to the Center for Occupational Hazards for comments, or get in touch with other occupational health and safety organizations such as OSHA or NIOSH.

4. Compare MSDSs of similar products in order to choose the product for which the most complete information is given and that contains the safest ingredients.

5. Use MSDS information to plan use of materials, product storage, and clean-up strategies.

6. File all MSDSs for easy access and make them available to all personnel.

Choosing safer products

Once you know as much as possible about the products you use, you can begin to select the safest brands. Here are some general principles about choosing safer products.

Choose products containing the least toxic chemicals. Use labels, MSDSs, and any other information about ingredients to compare product toxicity. Use this manual or other references (such as *Artist Beware*) that rate chemicals according to toxicity. Lacquer thinners, for example, may vary widely in the number and toxicity of their ingredients. Some lacquer thinner formulas contain solvents such as isophorone or trichloroethylene, which are far more toxic than necessary. Rather, choose lacquer thinners with safer ingredients. Or you might even find it possible to substitute plain acetone, which is much less toxic.

Choose water-based or latex products over solvent-containing products whenever possible. Solvents are among the most hazardous chemicals used in theater. Try to replace solvent-containing paints, inks, marking pens, adhesives, and the like. Watch for new and improved water-based products that are appearing on the market with increasing frequency. Be courageous and try these new products rather than relying on old techniques that require using more toxic materials.

Choose products that do not create dusts and mists. Try to buy products that are in solution rather than in powdered form, and avoid aerosol cans and spray products whenever possible so you can avoid inhalation hazards.

Avoid carcinogens. Contrary to popular opinion, there are relatively few carcinogens among the vast number of chemicals used in theater. Keep abreast of information about cancer-causing chemicals and replace products containing them.

Protective equipment

Even after you have investigated the products you use and have chosen the safest brands, you may still find that you must use some hazardous materials. In this case, you must find methods for reducing exposure to these materials. Such methods may vary from protective equipment (such as ventilation systems) to personal protective equipment (such as respirators and ear plugs).

Ventilation and respiratory protection

Providing proper ventilation is without doubt the single most important method of protecting theater workers from hazardous airborne materials. For occasional exposures to toxic substances or when ventilation is not available, you will find that respiratory protection in the form of face masks and respirators can be useful.

Both ventilation and respiratory protection are complex subjects and are treated in later chapters. Theater workers should be well versed in both these subjects.

Eye and face protection

Suitable eye and face protection in the form of goggles or shields will guard against a variety of hazards, including impact (from chipping, grinding), radiation (from welding, carbon arcs, lasers), and chemical splash (by solvents, acids). Such protective equipment should be used only if it meets the standards of the American National Standards Institute's *Practice for Occupational and Educational Eye and Face Protection* (ANSI Publication Z87.1). Be certain to choose eye protection appropriate to the hazard. A common mistake seen in theater shops, for example, is the use of chemical splash goggles for protection against grind-wheel particles.

If you use solvents or acids, an eye wash fountain should be a fixture in your shop. The fountain should be able to deliver fifteen minutes of water to rinse eyes while a physician is called. Small eye wash bottles are not satisfactory for this purpose and also may become contaminated with bacteria. Fountains also should be activated by a foot pedal, lever, or other mechanism that requires only a single movement to turn on the water and keep it running.

Do not wear contact lenses in shops where irritating liquids such as acids or solvents are used, or where dusts are present. Wearing contact lenses is usually forbidden in industrial situations involving eye hazards, even if protective goggles are worn.

Skin protection

Satisfactory chemical-resistant gloves have been developed for almost any use theater workers could imagine. They can be purchased in any length up to shoulder length, and in any thickness from paper-thin to very thick, and in many types of plastic and rubber to resist almost every kind of material. Theater workers, however, too often rely on surgical or household gloves that do not stand up well or that are permeable to some solvents and other materials.

Industrial glove manufacturers provide glove charts that show clearly which gloves resist various materials best. Manufacturers' catalogs will help you select gloves for other purposes such as protection from heat, radiation, and abrasion.

For protection from occasional splashes or very light exposure to chemicals, you may use special creams called "barrier creams." Some of these creams protect skin from solvents and oils, others from acids, and so on. Choose the right cream and use it exactly as directed.

Do not use harsh hand soap. Waterless skin cleaners are useful if their ingredients do not include solvents or other harsh chemicals. Never wash your hands with solvents such as turpentine or gasoline. Some people find that rubbing baby oil (mineral oil) on the skin and then washing with soap and water will remove many paints and inks. Using barrier cream should enable you to wash off paints with soap and water. However you decide to clean your skin, you should apply a good hand lotion afterward to replace any lost skin oils.

Hands are not the only part of the body for which skin protection has been developed. Aprons, leggings, leather or plastic clothing, shoes, and myriad special protective products are available. Remember, your skin's protective barrier is your first defense against many hazardous agents.

Ear protection

Ear-damaging levels of sound can be produced by the machinery in many shops, by musical instruments, and by sound equipment. OSHA has set limits for noise in the workplace, but the limits are often hard to enforce, and it takes special equipment to measure noise levels and to document exposure adequately. In general, if you need to raise you voice to be heard by someone two feet from you, you probably need hearing protection. Workers or students who are hearing impaired should be evaluated medically to determine if a noisy environment may further damage their hearing.

Eliminating or reducing noise is the best way to protect your hearing. There are many ways to damper or reduce machinery vibration and noise. Keep machinery oiled and in good repair: properly maintained machines run more quietly. When making new purchases, choose quieter brands of machinery.

If these methods do not lower noise levels sufficiently, then you should wear hearing protection such as ear plugs and muffs. A good selection of these appears in many safety catalogs.

Protective equipment rules

1. Use an expert appropriate to the job at hand when you plan for safety and health. For example, employ an industrial hygienist to survey your facilities for hazards, and engage an industrial ventilation engineer to plan shop ventilation.

2. Get expert advice from more than one source when choosing protective equipment or purchasing quieter machinery. Never rely primarily on equipment manufacturers or distributors for information.

3. Collect catalogs and other good sources for types of protective equipment such as *Best's Safety Directory*.

4. Determine if you or your students have special problems regarding protective equipment. For example, people with beards should not wear air-purifying respirators, and people with dermatitis may need special hand protection.

5. Enforce proper use of protective equipment. Ventilation systems are useless if they are not turned on; hearing is not protected by unused ear muffs.

6. Develop programs for regular repair, replacement, and maintenance of protective equipment.

Personal hygiene

One of the simplest and most often forgotten methods of avoiding exposure to toxic substances is practicing good hygiene in the workplace. Industrial experience has taught that even tiny amounts of certain toxic substances repeatedly ingested with food, brought home on clothing, or left on the skin can cause illness in workers or members of their families. These illnesses can be prevented easily if some basic rules are followed.

Do not eat, smoke, or drink or apply makeup in theater shops or other environments where there are toxic materials. Dust, after all, settles in coffee cups, sandwiches can absorb vapors, and hands can transfer substances to food and cigarettes for subsequent ingestion or inhalation. In addition, when substances are inhaled through a cigarette, the cigarette's heat can convert some materials into more hazardous forms.

Wear special work clothes and remove them after work. If possible, leave them in the workshop and wash them frequently and separately from other clothing. If the workplace is dusty, wear some form of hair covering (hair is a good dust collector). Do not wear loose clothing, scarves, ties, or jewelry. Pin back long hair.

Wash hands carefully after work, before eating, and before using the bathroom.

Storage and handling of materials

Many accidents, spills, and fires can be avoided by following rules for safe storage and handling of materials.

1. Make sure all containers, even those into which materials are transferred for storage, are labeled clearly, noting both their contents and hazards.

2. Use unbreakable containers whenever possible.

3. Organize storage wisely. For example, do not store large containers on high shelves where they are difficult to retrieve.

4. Store reactive chemicals separately. Check each product's MSDS for advice.

5. To prevent escape of dust or vapors, keep all containers closed except when using them.

6. In case of accidental skin contact with chemicals, wash affected area with lots of water and remove contaminated clothing. Check the product's label for additional first aid advice.

7. In case of eye accidents, rinse your eyes for at least fifteen minutes and get medical advice.

8. Do not use any cleaning methods that raise dust. Wet mop floors or sponge surfaces.

9. Dispose of waste or unwanted materials safely. Check product labels or contact manufacturers for advice. Do not pour solvents down drains. Pour nonpolluting aqueous liquids down the sink one at a time with lots of water. For large amounts of regularly produced wastes, engage a waste disposal service.

10. Clean spills immediately. If you use flammable liquids in the shop, prepare for spills by stocking chemical absorbants or other materials to collect spills, self-closing waste cans, and respiratory protection if needed. Empty waste cans daily.

11. Store quantities of flammable liquids greater than one quart in approved self-closing safety cans.

12. Do not store flammable or combustible materials near exits or entrances. Keep sources of sparks, flames, UV light, and heat as well as cigarettes away from flammable or combustible materials.

13. Keep an ABC-type fire extinguisher handy and train workers to use it.

Ventilation

Two kinds of ventilation—comfort and industrial—keep *theatergoers* comfortable and *theater workers* healthy.

Comfort ventilation

Comfort ventilation provides sufficient air movement and fresh air to avoid buildup of humidity, heat, and air pollution in buildings. This usually is accomplished by recirculating systems that use fans or blowers to circulate air from room to room throughout the building. On each recirculating cycle, some fresh air from outside is added and some recirculated air is exhausted. The amount of fresh air added usually varies from 5 to 30 percent, depending on how tightly insulated the building is and the vagaries of the particular ventilation system or its operator. Building engineers who operate ventilation systems often are encouraged to add as little fresh air as possible to reduce heating and cooling costs.

When insufficient amounts of fresh air are added, people in the building may complain of eye irritation, headaches, nausea, and other symptoms. Taken together, these sometimes are called the "sick-building syndrome." The symptoms are apparently caused by the accumulation of body heat, humidity, cigarette smoke, dust, formaldehyde, and other pollutants in the air.

Guidelines for acceptable indoor air quality in the form of ventilation standards have been developed by the American Society of Heating, Refrigerating, and Air-Conditioning Engineers (ASHRAE). In addition to these standards, most areas of the country have state codes or local codes or both that dictate the amount of ventilation that must be provided for public buildings, including theaters.

The ASHRAE Standards and many local codes are based on ventilation rates per person or per square foot. However, expressing rates in terms of the number of air exchanges per hour for a particular room provides an easier way to compare ventilation needs. For example, office spaces should have about four air exchanges per hour. Dressing rooms should have somewhat more, perhaps five exchanges per hour. Places of public assembly and seating areas should be provided up to ten exchanges per hour, and bathrooms about fifteen exchanges per hour ventilated to the outside. Lobbies and smoking areas may need even higher rates.

Theaters need especially good comfort ventilation. It must be efficient and quiet in order to accommodate audiences and performers, and it must comply with local health codes.

Industrial ventilation

Unlike lobbies and seating areas, which need comfort ventilation, workrooms and shops where toxic vapors, dusts, and chemicals become airborne require ventilation rates based on the amount of air pollution created. In fact, OSHA requires mechanical ventilation to protect workers in such locations. OSHA's *General Industry Standards* contains ventilation requirements.

Two types of industrial ventilation may be needed in theater shops: dilution ventilation and local exhaust ventilation.

Dilution ventilation. Dilution ventilation does exactly what its name implies. It dilutes or mixes contaminated workplace air with large volumes of clean air to reduce the amounts of contaminants to acceptable levels. Then the diluted mixture is exhausted (drawn by fans or other devices) from the workplace. Dilution systems usually consist of fresh air inlets (often having fans and systems for heating or cooling the air), and outlets (exhaust fans).

Although often cheap and easy to install, dilution ventilation has limitations. For example, only vapors or fumes of low toxicity, or very small amounts of moderately toxic vapors or fumes, are removed satisfactorily by dilution ventilation. Never use dilution ventilation to remove dusts, metal particles, or any highly toxic materials.

In theater shops, you might use dilution for areas where small amounts of solvent vapors are created, such as when you paint with latex paints (which usually contain between 5 and 15 percent solvents). Other good places for dilution ventilation include photographic darkrooms (black and white) and design studios where small amounts of turpentine, rubber cement, and the like are used. Do not use dilution ventilation in connection with woodworking, aerosol spraying, or other spray or airbrush operations.

Besides correct exhaust volume, successful dilution ventilation depends on the control and direction of air flow through the workspace. Careful positioning of the air inlets and outlets will ensure proper control. You should keep these basic principles in mind when you plan locations of inlets and outlets:

Figure 2   Good and bad dilution ventilation

BAD   **GOOD**

Source: Nancy Clark, Thomas Cutter, and Jean-Ann McGrane, *Ventilation: A Practical Guide* (New York: Center for Occupational Hazards, 1985), 29.

Move only clean air through a worker's breathing zone.

Position the workspace to avoid crossdrafts.

Locate the workspace and air inlets and outlets so that other workers in surrounding areas are not exposed.

Air inlets and outlets should be carefully and thoughtfully placed.

Local exhaust ventilation. Local exhaust ventilation, on the other hand, has a wide range of applications. It is the best means by which materials of moderate to high toxicity—gases, vapors, dusts, fumes—are removed from the workplace. Because local exhaust ventilation captures the contaminants at their source rather than after they have escaped into the room air, exhaust ventilation systems remove smaller amounts of air than dilution systems. It will be helpful to familiarize yourself with the advantages and disadvantages of both dilution and local exhaust ventilation.

Processes for which local exhaust ventilation are required include abrasive (sand) blasting; aerosol spraying; air brushing; color photographic processing and toning; grinding; heating pots of dye, glue, or wax; acid etching (for example, gobos); metal melting and casting; photolithography; plastic resin casting; screen printing; soldering; spray operations; welding; and woodworking.

Table 1

A comparison of dilution and local exhaust ventilation

DILUTION VENTILATION

Advantages	Disadvantages
1. Low equipment and installation costs.	1. Does not eliminate exposure to contaminated air.
2. Effective control for small amounts of low and medium toxicity solvents.	2. Should not be used for high toxicity vapors and gases.
3. Effective control for flammable and combustible gases and vapors.	3. Should not be used for large amounts of any gases and vapors.
4. Requires little maintenance.	4. Ineffective for particulates (dusts, metal particles, metal fumes).
	5. Requires large volumes of heated or cooled make-up air.
	6. Not effective for handling surges of gases or vapors or irregular emissions.
	7. People working close to contaminant source can still have large exposures.

LOCAL EXHAUST VENTILATION

Advantages	Disadvantages
1. Captures contaminants at source and removes them from workplace.	1. System design and installation can be expensive.
2. Can handle all types of contaminants, including dusts, metal fumes, etc.	2. Requires regular cleaning, inspection and maintenance.
3. Requires small amounts of make-up air since uses low exhaust volumes.	
4. Low on-going energy costs because of low amounts of make-up air.	
5. Only alternative for high toxicity airborne materials.	

Source: Nancy Clark, Thomas Cutter, and Jean-Ann McGrane, *Ventilation: A Practical Guide* (New York: Center for Occupational Hazards, 1984), 25.

Local exhaust systems consist of a *hood* enclosing the source of contamination or positioned very close to it to draw in the air; *ductwork* to carry away the contaminated air; possibly an *air-cleaner* or *collector* to filter or purify the air before it is released outside; and a *fan* to pull air through the system.

Figure 3   Typical local exhaust system

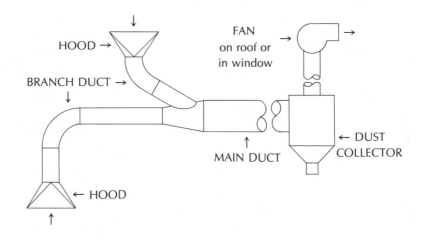

Source: PHILAPOSH.

Some of the rules to consider when choosing a local exhaust system include the following:

Put the hood close to the source. Surround it as completely as possible with the hood. The more the process is enclosed, the better the system will work.

Make sure the air flow is great enough to capture the contaminant. Keep in mind that dusts are heavy particles and require higher velocity air flow for capture than lighter vapors and gases.

Make sure that contaminated air flows away from your face, not past it.

Make sure that the exhausted air cannot reenter the shop through make-up air inlets, doors, windows, or other openings.

Make sure enough make-up air is provided to keep the system operating efficiently.

Types of hoods. A hood is the structure through which the contaminated air first enters the system. Hoods can vary from small dust-collecting types built around grind wheels to walk-in-sized spray booths. Several types are useful for theater shops.

Choosing ventilation systems

A number of systems can be used for common purposes in theater shops.

Dust-collecting systems. Most grind wheels, table saws, and other dust-producing machines sold today have dust-collecting hoods built into them. Some machines need only to be connected to portable dust collectors that can be purchased off the shelf. In other cases, stationary ductwork can be used to connect machines to dust collectors such as cyclones (which settle out particles) and bag houses (which capture particles on fabric filters). Theater workers should not work with dust-producing machines unless the machines are connected to dust collectors.

Spray booths. Spray booths from small table models to walk-in-sized or larger can be purchased or designed to fit the requirements of a particular shop. Some common uses for spray booths include spraying of paints, lacquers, adhesives, and other materials; plastic resin casting; paint stripping; and solvent cleaning of silk screens, objects, or costumes. Since spray paints and other sprays are likely to contain flammable solvents, the spray booth, its ducts and fans, and the area surrounding the booth must be made safe from explosion and fire hazards as required by the *General Industry Standards* and other local codes.

Movable exhaust systems. Also called "elephant trunk" systems, these flexible duct and hood arrangements are designed to remove fumes, gases, and vapors from processes such as welding, soldering, or any small tabletop processes that use solvents or solvent-containing products. Movable exhausts also can be equipped with pulley systems or mechanical arms designed to move hoods to almost any position.

Canopy hood systems. These hoods take advantage of the fact that hot gases rise. They are used over processes such as hot dye baths, wax and glue pots, and stove ranges. Unfortunately, they are sometimes installed above some theater shop worktables where they are not only ineffective because the hood is too far from the table, but where they are even dangerous because they draw contaminated air past the worker's face.

Slot hood systems. These systems draw gases and vapors across a work surface, away from the worker. Slot hood systems are good for any kind of bench work, including silk-screen printing, color photo developing, air brushing, and soldering. They are rather expensive to design and build, but provide a shop with surfaces on which many processes can be safely carried out.

Figure 4   Basic hood types

GRINDER HOOD
Encloses grind wheel and captures grinding dust.

Systems like this can be adapted to table saws, routers, and other machines.

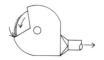

SPRAY BOOTH
Filters in rear of booth collect overspray.

For spraying, air brushing, resin casting, solvent use.

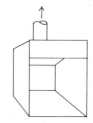

MOVABLE EXHAUST OR ELEPHANT
TRUNK HOOD
Hood positioned as close to work as possible.

For welding, soldering, sanding, other table-top work.

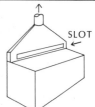

SLOT-TYPE or LATERAL HOOD

For photo developing, silk screening, air brushing, other bench work.

CANOPY or UPDRAFT HOOD
Not recommended if worker must bend over work.
Side curtain enclosure provides greater capture.

For dye baths, wax and glue pots, boiling liquids, hot gases.

Source: Ventilation, 35.

Special ventilation considerations

Theaters themselves, not just their workshops, also have special ventilation requirements. For example, stages should be equipped with systems that keep air
from flowing into the audience, an especially important system if special effects
such as smoke and fog are used on stage. Special fire protection systems may also
require the use of smoke exhaust fans and other systems. Theater ventilation also
must be very quiet so it does not distract audience attention.

Planning ventilation

Planning ventilation systems for theaters and large theater shops is usually too
complex for the in-house staff. Instead you should choose experts for each phase of
work. Carefully apprise these experts of your institution's needs before they begin.

In most cases, you first should choose an industrial hygienist to evaluate shop
and house hazards and recommend specific ventilation systems. Next select a
professional engineer experienced in industrial ventilation to design both dilution
and local exhaust ventilation systems. You may also want to employ a heating,
ventilating, and air conditioning (HVAC) engineer to help integrate the new ventilation systems into existing ones, or to upgrade comfort ventilation systems. Once the
experts have designed the systems, employ an appropriate contractor to install
them.

During planning and execution of ventilation jobs, theater administrators and
staff also should familiarize themselves with requirements for legal and proper
ventilation. You can accomplish this goal by consulting the *General Industry Standards* and the American Conference of Governmental Industrial Hygienists'
(ACGIH) *Industrial Ventilation: A Manual of Recommended Practice.*

Administrators and staff involved in planning ventilation should be particularly
careful to choose qualified experts. Engineering errors can result in very expensive
and time-consuming problems.

Administrators also should be leery of salesmen who tout products that appear
to solve ventilation problems cheaply by purifying contaminated air and returning it
to the workplace. Some of these devices, such as the negative-ion generator, are not
only useless in theater shops, but they actually can be harmful if they also generate
irritating ozone gas. Others, such as electrostatic precipitators, are very limited in
their uses and at best can be used only as adjuncts to traditional ventilation. For
example, they can successfully remove cigarette smoke particles (not the gases
produced by cigarettes) in lobbies and smoking areas.

Planning ventilation for small shops and individual studios is much less complicated. The Center for Occupational Hazards' book *Ventilation: A Practical
Guide* provides basic ventilation principles and calculations. Mechanically in-
clined theater workers should be able to use this manual to design and install
simple systems.

Checking the system

After a ventilation system has been installed, it should be checked to see that it is operating properly. If an engineer, industrial hygienist, or contractor worked on the job, he or she should make the initial check and recommend any changes necessary to meet design specifications. If experts were not consulted, you may decide to consult one at this stage. For example, air-flow devices can be used by an expert to measure air velocity and determine how well the system is functioning.

Even without the advice of an expert, some commonsense observations can be made:

Can you see the system pulling dusts and mists into it? If not, you might use artificial fog, smoke, or soap bubbles to check the system visually. When released in the area where the hood should be collecting, the fog or other substance should be drawn quickly and completely into the system.

Can you smell any gases or vapors? Sometimes placing inexpensive perfume near a hood can demonstrate a system's ability to collect vapors or it can show that exhausted air is returning to the workplace.

Do people working with the system complain of eye, nose, or throat irritation, or have other symptoms?

Is the fan noisy and irritating? A fan should not be so loud that people would rather endure the pollution than turn it on. Experts should be expected to work on the system until it is satisfactory in all ways.

Check ventilation systems periodically to see that they are continuing to work properly. Maintenance schedules for changing filters, cleaning ducts, and changing fan belts should be worked out and kept faithfully.

Air-purifying respirators

Theater craftspeople often incorrectly assume that it is simple to choose respiratory protection, and it is common to see someone confidently wearing an improper dust mask or respirator, damp handkerchief, or surgical mask that may in fact make the situation worse. Some general information about respiratory protection should help you choose proper equipment. More detailed information can be found in the Center for Occupational Hazards' data sheet "Air-Purifying Respirators for Theater Crafts."

Types of respirators. Respirators come in two basic types: air-supplied and air-purifying. Air-supplied respirators have systems for bringing fresh air to the wearer by means of pressurized tanks or compressors; they are complex and expensive.

Air-purifying respirators, on the other hand, use the wearer's breath to draw air through filters or chemical cartridges in order to purify it before it is inhaled. (There are also air-powered respirators that draw air through filters or cartridges for the wearer.) Most air-purifying respirators are priced in a range that theater workers will find practical.

When should respirators be used?. Adequate ventilation, not respirators, should be the primary means of controlling airborne toxic substances. OSHA regulations forbid using respirators for primary protection except when ventilation is being installed, maintained, or repaired, during emergencies, or if engineering controls are shown not to be feasible.

Respirator programs. If respirators are needed, the *employer is required* by OSHA to provide appropriate respiratory protection for employees and develop and implement a respiratory protection program (except in cases where respiratory protection is needed only very infrequently).

Schools and universities that allow students and teachers to wear respirators also should have *written* respirator programs. Written programs can be developed by following the guidelines in the NIOSH publication *Repiratory Protection . . . An Employer's Manual*. Such programs are required to consist of a number of components, including provisions for medical screening of people expected to wear respirators; for fit testing (testing to assure that a respirator fits a person's face and will not let contaminated air leak in); for cleaning, disinfecting, storing, and periodic inspection and repair of respirators; and for formal training in the use and limitations of respirators.

People who should *not* wear respirators include those who have physical problems, like certain heart or lung problems, and psychological problems, such as claustrophobia. There also may be temporary problems that would curtail respirator use, such as head colds and skin infections.

Other people should not wear a respirator because they cannot get a good seal against their skin. This allows air to bypass the filters or cartridges. For example, people with facial hair (beards and sideburns) or small faces (many women) cannot get a good seal or fit. Some companies now make smaller sizes for women.

How air-purifying respirators work

When air is drawn through a properly fitted respirator, it passes through either a filter or a cartridge. Filters are designed to trap particles such as dusts or metal fumes (which are fine particles created when metals are melted). Cartridges, on the other hand, trap vapors (such as those created when solvents evaporate) and gases (like ammonia). Different cartridges and filters are needed to trap dusts, fumes, gases, and vapors.

No filter or cartridge can remove all of a contaminant from the air. Instead, respirators are intended to *reduce* the amount of a particular substance to a relatively safe level, as determined by NIOSH. You should always use respirators approved by NIOSH because they have been proved to reduce contaminant levels.

When to replace filters and cartridges. Both filters and cartridges wear out and become ineffective with use. Filters clog progressively until breathing through them becomes difficult. Spent chemical cartridges, on the other hand, will allow the contaminant to pass through.

Chemical cartridges usually are considered spent after eight hours of use or two weeks after they have been exposed to air, whichever comes first. Chemical cartridges will wear out with time on their own, even if they are not used. For this reason, many brands of cartridges have an expiration date stamped on them.

You should test chemical cartridges before each use. For example, a simple test for organic vapor or spray paint cartridges is to pass an open bottle of iso-amyl acetate (banana oil) in front of the respirator when you first put it on. If you can detect the odor, replace the cartridge.

No filter or cartridge is designed to be effective when contaminants reach very high concentrations. At such high concentrations, more contaminants pass through cartridges and filters than is desirable, and they will wear out in a shorter time— sometimes in minutes.

Chemicals against which respirators are effective. NIOSH tests and approves filters and cartridges only for specific kinds of airborne contaminants. You should familiarize yourself with abbreviations for some of the filters and cartridges that theater craftspeople might use.

Table 2

Contaminants

| | Abbreviations for | |
	Cartridge	Filter
Acid gas: gases rising from acids, bleaches, or some photographic chemicals.	AG	
Ammonia: cleaners, diazo copier chemicals.	NH3	
Organic vapor: evaporating solvents.	OV	
Formaldehyde: plywood, urea formaldehyde glues.	FOR	
Paint, lacquer, and enamel mist: spray, airbrush, aerosol paints	PLE*	
Pesticides: sprays.	PEST	
Asbestos: should not need to be used.		A
*Dusts**:* powders or dust from sanding, sawing, etc.		D
*Mists**:* water-based spray products.		M
*Fumes**:* from heating, casting, melting metals.		F

*An organic vapor cartridge with a spray paint pre-filter.

**Designed as respiratory protection against dusts, mists, and metal fumes having a permissible exposure level (measured as time weighted average) not less than 0.05 milligrams per cubic meter or dusts and mists having an air contamination level not less than 2 million particles per cubic foot of air.

Source: "Air Purifying Respirators" (COH, 1982).

Never use air-purifying respirators in oxygen-deficient atmospheres, such as when gas is released in a confined space or in firefighting. Also do not use them against chemicals that are of an extremely hazardous nature, or lack sufficient warning properties (smell or taste), are highly irritating, or are not effectively absorbed on filter or cartridge material. Included among these are hot or burning wax vapors (acrolein and other hazardous decomposition products), carbon monoxide, methyl (wood) alcohol, isocyanates (from foaming or casting polyurethane), nitric acid, ozone, methyl ethyl ketone peroxide (used to harden polyester resins), and phosgene gas (created when chlorinated hydrocarbon solvents come into contact with heat or flame).

Air-purifying respirators also should not be used against cancer-causing substances, since they merely reduce rather than eliminate toxic exposure.

Choosing a respirator

The choice of a respirator generally involves selecting among half- and full-faced respirators. Respirators with large capacity canisters are designed for heavily contaminated air. (To handle more heavily contaminated atmospheres, use air-supplied respirators.) Use full-faced respirators when the contaminant is also an eye hazard or irritant.

It is important that you know precisely what contaminant is in the air and its physical form (gas, vapor, particle, fume) before you choose filters and cartridges. There are cartridges and filters for each substance and process you may work with.

The yellow pages of any good-sized city's telephone book will list distributors of respirators under the heading of safety equipment. Or consult a catalog such as *Best's Safety Directory*. Names and addresses of a few suppliers are listed below.

American Optical Corp.
Safety Products Division
14 Mechanic Street
Southbridge, MA 01550

Mine Safety Appliances Co.
600 Penn Center Blvd.
Pittsburgh, PA 15235

North Safety Products
2000 Plainfield Pike
Cranston, RI 02920

Scott Aviation/Div. Figgie Int'l.
2225 Erie St.
Lancaster, NY 14086

OH and SP Division/3M
220-7W, 3M Center
St. Paul, MN 55144

Wilson Safety Products
P.O. Box 622
Reading, PA 19603

Respirator care. At the end of a work period, clean your respirator. Store it out of sunlight in a sealable plastic bag. Respirators *never* should be hung on hooks in the open or left on counters in the shop.

If a respirator is shared, it should be cleaned and disinfected between users. Inspect respirators carefully and periodically for wear and damage.

Table 3

Selection chart for filters and cartridges

Substance or process	Cartridge	Filter
Aerosol sprays—*see* spraying		
Air Brush		
solvent-containing	PLE	
water-based		M
Ammonia	NH3	
Asbestos (protects only against asbestosis)		A
Dusts: wood, plaster, clay, fiber, and other toxic dusts		D or DM
Dye powders		D or DM
Fiberglass wool or insulation		D or DM
Formaldehyde	FOR	
Hydrochloric (muriatic) or acids	AG	
Lacquers and fixatives		
if evaporating	OV	
if sprayed	PLE	
Metal melting or casting		F or DMF
Metal fumes from welding (will not protect wearer from welding gases)		DMF
Metal powder		D or DM
Paint strippers (solvent-containing)	OV	
Photo-printmaking solvents (evaporating)	OV	
Pigments (powdered)		D or DM
Plastic cements and glues	OV	
Plastic resin casting (except for urethane)	OV	
Plastic sanding, grinding, and cutting (except for urethane and PVC)	OV *and*	D or DM
PVC (polyvinyl chloride) sanding and grinding	AG/OV *and*	D
Silk screen wash ups	OV	
Soldering		DMF
with acid, fluoride, and zinc chloride fluxes	AG *and*	DMF
Solvents (evaporating)	OV	
Spray adhesives	PLE	
Spraying toxic water-based paints, dyes, and other materials		DM
Spraying solvent-containing paints, dyes and other materials	PLE	

Reprinted from "Air Purifying Respirators" (COH, 1982).

III

The hazards

Paints, inks, pigments, and dyes

Today almost every kind of paint, ink, pigment, and dye is used in theater. For scene painting, traditional caseins have been supplemented by a host of consumer paints, artists' materials, and industrial paints. Costumers now use dyes designed for the new synthetic fabrics, fabric paints, silk-screen inks, and many more new materials. When something new appears on the market, it is quickly adapted for use in theater.

Unfortunately, the hazards of both traditional and new materials often are not sufficiently understood by theater craftspeople and teachers.

What are paints and inks?

Paints and inks are made up of two components: a pigment and a vehicle, or base. The most common vehicles are solvents and water. Vehicles usually also contain binders, such as oils, casein, and polymer emulsions, and additives, such as stabilizers (to keep ingredients in suspension), preservatives, plasticizers, antioxidants, and fillers. The hazards of many of these chemical additives have not been well researched. However, it is assumed that the most potentially hazardous ingredients in paints are solvents and pigments. A more complete discussion of the hazards of different types of paint can be found in the Center for Occupational Hazards' data sheet "Paints Used in Theater Crafts."

Pigments

The hazards of pigments have been known since 1713 when Ramazzini described illnesses associated with pigment grinding. A more recent study of commonly used pigments found twenty-four that were either toxic or had cancer-causing effects. Since several hundred pigments are used in art and craft products, dividing them into categories helps make the subject less intimidating: basically, most can be classified as inorganic or synthetic organic.

Table 4

Inhalation hazards of premixed paints and inks

The following hazards and precautions apply to paint and ink techniques, such as brushing and dipping, which do not cause pigments and vehicles to become airborne. Spraying, air-brushing, and similar methods are far more hazardous and require local exhaust systems, such as spray booths.

Acrylic paints (water-based) release small amounts of formaldehyde and ammonia during drying. Can cause respiratory irritation and allergies. Formaldehyde has caused cancer in animals. Provide a small amount of dilution ventilation, such as a window exhaust fan.

Acrylic paints (solvent-based) contain solvents and are cleaned up and thinned with solvents. Provide dilution ventilation.*

Artist's oils do not contain volatile ingredients but are thinned and cleaned up with toxic solvents such as turpentine and paint thinner. Provide dilution ventilation*, such as a window exhaust fan. Some people also work thickly with paints using no thinners, cleaning brushes with baby oil followed by soap and water. No special ventilation is needed if solvents are not used.

Alkyd paints contain solvents and must be cleaned up and thinned with solvents. Provide dilution ventilation.*

Commercial oil enamels and paints contain a variety of solvents and are thinned and cleaned up with solvents. Provide dilution ventilation.*

Commercial latex paints, contrary to common belief, usually contain between 5 and 15 percent solvents. Some very hazardous solvents, such as glycol ethers, have been found in latex paints. Provide dilution ventilation.*

Marking Pens. Permanent markers contain solvents of varying toxicity. Watercolor markers are safer and are usually water- or water-and-alcohol-based. Provide dilution ventilation for solvent-containing markers.*

Silk-screen inks (solvent-based) contain solvents. Screens must be cleaned with solvents, resulting in heavy exposure for artists in unventilated studios. Provide local exhaust ventilation for printing area (slot hoods), drying racks, and screen wash area.

Silk-screen inks (water-based) are often specially retarded (slow drying) acrylics. They are an excellent alternative to more hazardous solvent-based inks. Provide some dilution ventilation.*

Watercolor, caseins, tempera, and poster paints often contain small amounts of preservatives such as formaldehyde, paraformaldehyde, or phenol. These are generally the safest types of paint. Exhaust ventilation usually is not needed.

*Ventilation rates will depend on the type and amount of solvent vaporized. See *Ventilation*.

Table 5

Hazards of Pigments

Common name	CI pigment name	
Lead pigments: do not use.		
Chrome green	Pigment Green	15
Chrome yellow	Pigment Yellow	34
Flake white	Pigment White	1
Molybdate (moly) orange	Pigment Red	104
Naples yellow	Pigment Yellow	41
Automobile paints and metal primers also often contain lead.		
Pigments associated with cancer: replace or use with great caution.		
Cadmium yellow (also other cadmium colors)	Pigment Yellow	37
Chrome green (also other chrome colors)	Pigment Green	15
Diarylide (benzidine) yellow*	Pigment Yellow	12
Lithol red	Pigment Red	49
Phthalocyanine (phthalo) blue*	Pigment Blue	15
Phthalocyanine (phthalo) green*	Pigment Green	7
Zinc yellow	Pigment Yellow	36
Pigments with moderate hazards: use with caution		
Burnt and raw umber	Pigment Brown	7
Cobalt green	Pigment Green	19
Cobalt violet (cobalt phosphate)	Pigment Violet	14
Cobalt yellow	Pigment Yellow	40
Manganese blue	Pigment Blue	33
Manganese violet	Pigment Violet	16
Toluidine (hansa) red	Pigment Red	3
Pigments with no significant hazards: use with normal care.		
Burnt and raw sienna	Pigment Brown	6
English red	Pigment Red	101
Ivory black	Pigment Black	9
Mars black	Pigment Black	11
Mars yellow (and all other Mars colors)	Pigment Yellow	41
Prussian blue	Pigment Blue	27
Titanium white	Pigment White	6
Ultramarine blue	Pigment Blue	29

*Contaminated with PCBs.

Inorganic pigments come from the earth (ochres, for example), or they are prepared from metals or minerals (cadmium red or lead white, for example). The toxic effects of these pigments are fairly well known. The lead-containing colors are especially toxic. Although lead is banned from most consumer wall paints, products such as automobile, boat, and artist's paints are exempt from the law and may contain lead.

Synthetic organic pigments are synthesized from organic chemicals. Examples are phthalo blue and the fluorescent colors. There are literally hundreds of these synthetic pigments, and only a small percentage of them have been studied for toxicity or long-term hazards. Of those that have been studied, some have been shown to be toxic, and some are know to cause cancer. Some synthetic pigments also are hazardous because they contain highly toxic impurities such as cancer-causing PCBs. These impurities are unwanted byproducts created during manufacture.

Dyes

Industrial experience has demonstrated tragically that many dyes can harm those who use them. One group of dyes (those chemically related to the chemical benzidine) have been shown to cause bladder cancer, and many other dyes have caused severe allergies. The hazards of most dyes, however, are unknown because only a few of the several thousand commercial dyes have been tested for long-term effects. One small group of dyes—food dyes—has been tested for long-term effects. Of the nearly one hundred food dyes available in 1950, only nine are still considered safe and three of these are undergoing further testing. Prudence dictates handling all dyes cautiously.

Almost all dyes used today are synthetic organic chemicals. The very first synthetic dyes were made from coal-tar aniline. Some companies still use the word "aniline" to identify their dyes, but—it is hoped—the word only means "synthetic," since real aniline dyes are too toxic to be used safely in theater.

Chemically, dyes can be separated into classes. Each class reacts with certain fibers in certain ways. For example, direct dyes are used for cotton, linen, and rayon, and they usually need to be applied using hot-water baths containing salt to react properly with the fabrics.

Dyes in the same class usually have *some* hazards in common, but in addition they may—and usually do—possess some individual hazards. This is because dyes in the same class bind themselves to fibers in the same way chemically, so the hazards related to the fiber-binding part of the dye molecule are similar within each class of dye. But the rest of the molecule may vary from dye to dye and its effects on health may vary correspondingly. A more complete discussion of the hazards of dyes can be found in the Center for Occupational Hazards' data sheet "Dye Hazards and Precautions."

Table 6

Hazards of dyes by class

Acid dyes. Usually used on silk or wool. Often require addition of dye-assisting chemicals or mordants or both. Probably one of the least acutely toxic classes, although some carcinogenic food dyes and benzidine dyes belong to this class.

Azoic or Naphthol dyes. Usually used on cellulosic fibers, acetate, triacetate, and polyester. These dyes have been reported to cause severe allergies and skin reactions, including depigmentation.

Basic dyes. Usually used on wool, silk, and some synthetics. Fluorescent dyes usually belong to this class. Allergic reactions to some of these dyes have been reported, and some are considered carcinogens.

Direct dyes. Usually used on cotton, linen, and rayon applied from hot baths that contain salt. Usually present few acute hazards but the majority of cancer-causing benzidine dyes are found in this class.

Disperse dyes. Usually used on water-repellent fibers such as triacetate, nylon, polyester, and polyacrylonitrile (Dynel, Orlan, and Arlan). While other dyes have caused dermatitis on direct skin contact, only disperse dyes have caused widespread dermatitis from contact with the finished product. Use with great caution and for products other than apparel.

Fiber-reactive dyes. Also called "cold water," "batik," or "Procion" dyes, some forms will dye cellulosic fibers while others will dye wool, silk, and nylon. Bulk containers of these dyes are labeled with warnings about allergic respiratory reactions that some distributors fail to transfer to labels of smaller packages. Use special caution to avoid inhaling these dyes or getting them on your skin.

Vat dyes. Most vat dyes are used for cellulosic fibers, while some are suitable for wool and acetate fibers. The dyeing process usually requires the use of lye or caustic soda either in the bath or as a pretreatment for the dye. Pretreated dyes are caustic to handle or inhale. Another potential hazard involves vat dyes' need for oxidation after they have been applied. Air oxidizes some dyes, but others require treatment with dichromate salts that can cause allergies. Some vat dyes themselves also have been reported to cause allergies. Extreme care should be exercised if they are used. Wear goggles. Some vat dyes are sold as pigments; using these is not recommended.

Other dye products

All-purpose or union dyes. These common household dyes mix two or more classes of dyes together with salt so that a wide variety of fabrics may be dyed. Only the dye that is specific for the cloth immersed is "taken" by the fabric. The number of dyes mixed obviously increases the potential hazard and some products contain the benzidine dyes. If these products must be used, liquid products should be chosen and used only occasionally, with much caution.

Other chemicals need to be added to some dye baths to help them react properly. These chemicals are often called dye-assisting or mordanting chemicals.

Table 7

Hazards of mordants and dye-assisting chemicals

Alum (potassium aluminum sulfate). Some people may be allergic to alum, but no special precautions are needed when using it.

Ammonia* (ammonium hydroxide). Avoid concentrated solutions. Household-strength ammonia is diluted and less hazardous. Inhalation of its vapors can cause respiratory and eye irritation.

Ammonium alum (ammonium aluminum sulfate). Hazards are the same as those of alum.

Caustic soda* (lye, sodium hydroxide). Very corrosive to the skin, eyes, and respiratory tract.

Chlorine bleach* (household bleach, 5 percent sodium hypochlorite). Corrosive to the skin, eyes, throat, and mucous membranes. Mixing with ammonia results in the release of extremely poisonous nitrogen trichloride gas. Mixing with acids releases highly irritating chlorine gas.

Copper sulfate* (blue vitriol). May cause allergies and irritation of the skin, eyes, and upper respiratory tract. Chronic exposure to copper sulfate dust can cause ulceration and perforation of the nasal septum.

Cream of tartar (potassium acid tartrate). No significant hazards.

Ferrous sulfate* (copperas). Slightly irritating to skin, eyes, nose, and throat. No special precautions necessary.

Formic acid* (methanoic acid). Highly corrosive to eyes and mucous membranes. May cause mouth, throat, and nasal ulcerations.

Glauber's salt (sodium sulfate). Slightly irritating to skin, eyes, nose, and throat.

Oxalic acid*. Skin and eye contact may cause severe corrosion and ulceration. Inhalation can cause severe respiratory irritation and damage. Wear gloves and goggles.

Potassium dichromate* (potassium bichromate, chrome). Skin contact may cause allergies, irritation, and ulceration. Chronic exposure can cause respiratory allergies. A suspect carcinogen. Wear gloves and goggles.

Salt* (sodium chloride). Some all-purpose dyes contain enough to be toxic to children by ingestion. No other significant hazards.

Sodium carbonate*. Corrosive to the skin, eyes, and respiratory tract.

Sodium hydrosulfite* (sodium dithionite). Irritating to the skin and respiratory tract. Stored solutions decompose to release irritating sulfur dioxide gas. Mixture with acids will release large amounts of sulfur dioxide gas.

continued

Table 7, *continued*

Hazards of mordants and dye-assisting chemicals

Sulfuric acid* (oleum). Highly corrosive to skin and eyes. Vapors can damage respiratory system. Heating generates irritating sulfur dioxide gas.

Tannin* (tanic acid). Slight skin irritant. Causes cancer in animals. Handle with care.

Tin chloride* (tin, stannous chloride). Irritating to the skin, eyes, and respiratory tract.

Urea. No significant hazards.

Vinegar (dilute acetic acid). Glacial (pure) acetic acid is highly corrosive and the vapors are irritating. Vinegar (about 5 percent acetic acid) is safer. Mildly irritating to skin and eyes.

*Can be poisonous if ingested. Keep out of reach of children.

Pigment and dye identification

Companies selling theater paints, inks, pigments, and dyes list colors in many ways, sometimes using traditional names or simple colors, sometimes using fanciful names designed to attract customers. As a result, it is almost impossible to know the actual color chemicals to which these names refer. For example, catalogs often list a scene paint identified as "chrome yellow." Chrome yellow is defined in the dictionary as lead chromate. Lead chromate is highly toxic, a human carcinogen, and can cause birth defects. If chrome yellow scene paint really contains lead chromate, workers who spray or sand it should be under strict medical surveillance and subject to other protective measures as established by the OSHA Lead Standard.

Even if chrome yellow scene paint is *not* lead chromate, theater workers still should know what it *is*, because each different yellow pigment has different properties and potential hazards. For example, if a yellow paint's pigment is actually cadmium yellow, use caution because cadmium yellow is a suspect carcinogen and should not be heated because the cadmium will fume. If it is cobalt yellow, it can cause an illness called methemoglobinemia. If it is diarylide yellow, it is contaminated with cancer-causing PCBs. If it is Mars yellow, it has no significant hazards. And so on.

The answer to this identification problem is simple. All commercial pigments and dyes are assigned "Color Index" (CI) names and numbers. These CI identifications are recognized internationally, and pigment, dye, ink, and paint users should ask distributors to provide CI names or numbers. Many responsible manufacturers of fine-arts products already provide this service for customers, and theater product makers should be expected to follow suit.

Once they are identified, colors' chemical hazards can be investigated. Such sources as *Artist Beware* and the Center for Occupational Hazards' data sheet "Dye Hazards and Precautions" will be useful, but information on many dyes and some synthetic pigments will not be found because not all have been studied. Treat untested substances with great caution.

Rules for using paints, inks, and dyes

1. Obtain Material Safety Data Sheets (MSDSs) on all paint and dye products. If pigments and dyes are not identified by their CI names or numbers, ask your supplier for this information.

2. Use MSDSs and product labels to identify the hazards of any toxic solvents, acids, or other chemicals in dyes, paints, inks, mordants, or other materials.

3. Use water-based products whenever possible.

4. Buy premixed paints and dyes if possible. Dyes packaged in packets that dissolve when dropped unopened into hot water also can be handled safely. Pigments and dyes are most hazardous and inhalable in a dry powdered state.

Figure 5   Glove box for mixing powders

Source: Ventilation, 14.

5. Weigh or mix dye powders or other toxic powders where local exhaust ventilation is available, or use a glove box.

6. Avoid dusty procedures. Sanding dry paints, sprinkling dry pigments or dyes on wet paint or glue, and other techniques that raise dust should be discontinued or performed in a local exhaust environment. If you use such processes without ventilation, choose pigments known to be of low toxicity, do not use dyes, wear a toxic dust respirator, and use wet-mop cleaning procedures.

7. Choose brushing and dipping techniques over spray methods whenever possible.

8. Spray paints or dyes only under local exhaust conditions, such as in a spray booth. A proper respirator (dust and mist respirator for water-based paints; paint, lacquer, and enamel mist [PLE] respirator for solvent-containing products) may provide additional protection.

9. Avoid skin contact with paints and pigments by wearing gloves or using barrier creams. Use gloves with dyes. Wash off paint splashes with safe cleaners like baby oil followed by soap and water, non-irritating waterless hand cleaners, or plain soap and water. Never use solvents or bleaches to remove splashes from your skin.

10. Wear protective clothing, including a full-length smock or coveralls. Leave these garments in your studio to avoid bringing dusts home. Wear goggles if you use caustic dyes or corrosive chemicals.

11. Work on easy-to-clean surfaces and wipe up spills immediately. Wet mop and sponge floors and surfaces. Do not sweep.

12. Avoid ingestion of materials by not eating, smoking, or drinking in your workplace. Never use your lips to make a point on a brush; do not hold brush handles in your teeth. Never use cooking utensils for dyeing. A pot that seems clean can be porous enough to hold hazardous amounts of residual dye. Wash your hands before eating or smoking.

13. Keep containers of paint, powdered dyes, pigments, and solvents closed except when you are using them.

14. Follow all solvent safety rules if you use solvent-containing products.

15. Arrange for regular blood tests for lead if you use lead-containing paints or pigments.

Solvents

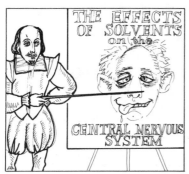

What are solvents?

The term "solvents" refers to liquid organic chemicals used to dissolve solid materials. Examples of solvents are turpentine, acetone, kerosene, and lacquer thinner. Solvents are used widely in the theater because in liquid form they dissolve materials like paints, resins, and plastics, and because they evaporate (form an airborne vapor) quickly and cleanly.

All solvents are toxic. They are hazardous in both their liquid and vapor state. *There are no safe solvents*, but some are more toxic than others.

In general, solvents can cause skin disease, irritate the eyes and respiratory tract, cause a narcotic effect on the nervous system, and damage internal organs such as the liver and kidneys. In addition, some solvents are especially hazardous to specific organs or can cause specific diseases such as cancer.

A more detailed treatment of solvents can be found in the Center for Occupational Hazards' data sheet "Solvents Used in Theater Crafts."

Skin disease

All solvents can dissolve the skin's protective barrier of oils, causing a kind of dermatitis. In addition, some solvents can cause severe burning and irritation of the skin. Others may cause no symptoms, but may penetrate the skin, enter the blood stream, travel through the body, and damage other organs.

Irritation of the eyes and respiratory tract

All solvent vapors can irritate and damage the sensitive membranes of the eyes, nose, and throat. Inhaled deeply, solvent vapors also can damage lungs. The airborne concentration at which irritation occurs varies from solvent to solvent. Often workers are unaware of solvents' effects at low concentrations. Their only symptoms may be increased frequency of colds and respiratory infections.

At higher concentrations symptoms are more severe and may include nose bleeds, tearing, and sore throat. Inhaling very high concentrations may lead to severe disorders including chemical pneumonia. Liquid solvents splashed in the eyes can cause severe eye damage.

Effect on the nervous system

All solvents can affect the brain or central nervous system (CNS), causing "narcosis." Immediate symptoms of this effect on the CNS may include dizziness, irritability, headaches, fatigue, and nausea. At progressively higher doses, the symptoms may proceed from apparent drunkenness to unconsciousness and death. Years of chronic exposure to solvents can cause permanent CNS damage, resulting in memory loss, apathy, depression, insomnia, and other psychological problems that are hard to distinguish from the same problems with other causes.

Solvents also may damage the peripheral nervous system (PNS), which is the system of nerves leading from the spinal cord to the arms and legs. The symptoms caused by this PNS damage are numbness and tingling in the extremities, weakness, and paralysis. Some solvents such as n-hexane (found in rubber cement and many spray products) can cause a combination of CNS and PNS effects, resulting in a disease with symptoms similar to multiple sclerosis.

Damage to internal organs

There is considerable variation in the kinds and degrees of harm different solvents can do to internal organs. Many solvents can damage the liver and kidney as these organs attempt to detoxify and eliminate the solvents from the body. One solvent, carbon tetrachloride, has such a devastating effect on the liver, especially in combination with alcohol ingestion, that many deaths have resulted from its use.

Many solvents also can alter heart rhythm, even causing heart attacks at high doses. Methylene chloride, a solvent often found in spray-can products and plastics adhesives, is especially capable of damaging the heart because it also metabolizes (breaks down) in the blood stream to form heart-stressing carbon monoxide. Methylene chloride is reputed to have caused a heart attack in a young woman wardrobe attendant who was using a shoe spray on a large costume in a small unvented room.

Some solvents also are known to cause cancer in humans or animals. Benzene can cause leukemia. Carbon tetrachloride can cause liver cancer. Many experts suspect that all chlorinated solvents (those with "chloro" or "chloride" in their names) may be carcinogens.

Reproductive hazards and birth defects

The effects of solvents on reproduction have not been well researched. Those studies that do exist show there is reason for concern. For example, two types of solvents—the cellosolves (which are found in many photographic chemicals, liquid cleaning products, some paints and inks, and aerosol sprays) and the diglycidal ethers (found in epoxy resin products)—atrophy animals' testicles and cause birth defects. Also, Scandinavian studies show higher rates of miscarriages, birth defects, and other problems among workers who were exposed to solvents on their jobs. A more complete discussion of this subject can be found the Center for Occupational Hazards' data sheet "Reproductive Hazards in the Arts and Crafts."

In addition, recent studies of one of the least toxic solvents—grain alcohol— have shown that babies born to drinking mothers may be of low birth weight, have varying degrees of mental retardation, and suffer from other abnormalities. Cautious doctors counsel women planning pregnancies to avoid both alcohol and solvent exposure.

Explosion and fire hazards

Solvents also cause many fires and explosions. There are two ways of measuring a solvent's capacity to burn and explode.

1. Flash point—the lower a solvent's flash point, the lower the temperature at which its vapors can ignite in the presence of a spark or flame. Solvents such as acetone and hexane, whose flash points are below room temperature, are especially dangerous.

2. Vapor pressure—the higher a solvent's vapor pressure, the more quickly it can convert from a liquid to a vapor (evaporate). Solvents with high vapor pressure are dangerous because flammable vapors ignite readily.

The chlorinated hydrocarbons are usually not flammable (so they have no flash point), but on heating or burning their decomposition produces dangerous phosgene gas.

As a result, you generally should isolate solvents from sources of heat, sparks, flame, and static electricity.

Chemical classes of solvents

All solvents fall into various classes of chemicals. A class is a group with similar molecular structures and chemical properties. Important classes of solvents are alcohols, aliphatic hydrocarbons, aromatic hydrocarbons, chlorinated hydrocarbons, esters, ethers, cellosolves, and ketones.

Rules for solvent use

1. Try to find replacements for solvent-containing products. More and better water-based products are being developed as technology improves. Keep abreast of developments in new materials.

2. Use the least toxic solvent possible. Substitute safer solvents from the same class whenever possible. The table notes the safest solvent in each major class. Research the solvents in the products you use and choose products containing safer solvents.

3. Avoid breathing vapors. Use solvents in areas where local exhaust ventilation is available. Very small amounts of solvents or solvent-containing products may be used with dilution ventilation. Use self-closing waste cans for solvent-soaked rags, keep containers closed when not in use, and observe other practices designed to reduce solvent evaporation.

4. Avoid skin contact. Wear gloves for heavy solvent exposure and use barrier creams for incidental light exposures. Wash off splashes immediately with water. Never clean hands with solvents.

5. Protect eyes from solvents. Wear protective goggles whenever solvents are poured or there is a chance a splash may occur. Only use solvents where an eye wash fountain or other source of water for flushing eyes is present.

6. Protect against fire, explosion, and decomposition hazards. Never smoke or permit flames or sparks near solvents. Heat and ultraviolet light should not be used near chlorinated hydrocarbons. Local exhaust ventilation fans for solvent vapors must be explosion-proof.

7. Be prepared for spills. If spills of large amounts are likely, use chemical solvent absorbers sold by most major chemical supply houses.

Table 8

Common solvents and their hazards

Currently or in the past, the solvents listed here have been used in theater crafts products. They are grouped according to their chemical class. Chemicals in the same class often have similar solvent properties, so you may readily find safer substitutes by using the table. If you need information on solvents not included here, consult the bibliography for additional sources.

Solvent class	TLV (ppm)	FP (°F)	VP (mm Hg
Alcohols			
ethanol (denatured, ethyl or grain alcohol)	1000	55	43
methanol (wood or methyl alcohol)	200	52	97
n-propyl alcohol	200	59	15
isopropyl alcohol (rubbing alcohol)	400	53	33
isoamyl alcohol (fuse oil)	100	109	2
Aliphatic hydrocarbons			
n-hexane	50	–7	124
heptane	400	25	40
benzine	100	varies	varies
petroleum naptha	100	–50	40
gasoline	300	100–150	varies
VM&P naptha	300	20–55	2–20

Abbreviations:

chem	chemical	irr	irritating to eyes, skin, or
CNS	central nervous system		upper respiratory system
CVS	cardiovascular system	mm Hg	millimeters of mercury
derm	dermatitis	perm	permanent
FP	flash point in degrees	PNS	peripheral nervous system
	Fahrenheit	ppm	parts per million
GI	gastro-intestinal system	resp sys	respiratory system

skin* the substance is absorbed
through the skin
TLV threshold limit value set by
American Conference of
Governmental Industrial
Hygienists (ACGIH) 1984–85
URT upper respiratory tract
VP vapor pressure

Comments	Organs affected	Symptoms
One of safer classes		
Least toxic in class; identify denaturant	eyes, nose, skin, CNS	irr, headache, drowsiness, fatigue, tremors
Use ethanol when possible; skin*	eyes, skin, CNS	blurred vision, optic nerve damage, blindness
skin*	eyes, skin, CNS, URT	irr, drowsiness, derm
One of least toxic in class	eyes, skin, URT, CNS	irr drowsiness, dizziness
skin*	eyes, skin, URT, CNS	irr, narcosis, derm, diarrhea
Do not use; extremely flammable	skin, URT, CNS, PNS	irr, peripheral neuropathy, perm CNS damage
Good substitute for n-hexane	skin, resp sys, lungs, PNS	narcosis, derm, nausea, chemical pneumonia
Can contain hexanes, pentanes and/or VM&P naptha; use TLV of Stoddard solvent	skin, CNS, lungs	irr, narcosis, derm
Mixture of aliphatic hydrocarbons; may contain benzene; use TLV of Stoddard solvent; extremely flammable	eyes, skin, URT, CNS, lungs	irr, narcosis, derm
Do not use; may contain benzene and/or lead; extremely flammable	skin, URT, CNS	irr, derm, narcosis, chem pneumonia, pulmonary edema
One of least toxic	skin, CNS, lungs	irr, derm, narcosis

continued

Table 8, *continued*

Common solvents and their hazards

Solvent class	TLV (ppm)	FP (°F)	VP (mm Hg)
Aliphatic hydrocarbons *(continued)*			
mineral spirits	200	86–105	0.8
kerosene	none	100–165	varies
Aromatic hydrocarbons			
benzene (benzol)	10	12	75
toluene (toluol)	100	40	22
xylene (xylol)	100	81	9
styrene (vinyl benzene)	50	90	4.5
Chlorinated hydrocarbons			
carbon tetrachloride	5	none	91
chloroform	10	none	160
methylene chloride	100	none	350
methyl chloroform (1, 1, 1-trichloro ethane)	350	none	100
trichloroethylene	50	none	58
perchloroethylene (tetrachloroethylene)	50	none	14

Comments	Organs affected	Symptoms
TLV from Patty; odorless paint thinner or mineral spirits with reduced aromatics preferred	skin, CNS, lungs	irr, derm, narcosis
	skin, lungs, URT, CNS	irr, narcosis, lung hemorrhage, chem pneumonia
Try to avoid as a class		
Do not use; cancer agent; skin* extremely flammable	skin, CNS, blood, chromosomes, liver, kidneys	derm, narcosis, leukemia, aplastic anemia
skin*	CNS, liver, URT, kidneys, skin	derm, narcosis, muscular weakness, liver & kidney damage
skin*	skin, URT, CNS, liver, GI, blood	irr, narcosis, derm, stomach pain
	skin, CNS, liver, lungs	irr, derm, narcosis, liver & blood damage
Try to avoid as a class. May produce phosgene gas and other toxics when heated or exposed to ultraviolet radiation.		
Do not use; suspect cancer agent; skin*	skin, CNS, liver, kidneys, stomach	irr, narcosis, hepatitis, kidney failure, stomach pain
Do not use; suspect cancer agent; skin*	skin, heart, liver, kidneys, eyes, CNS	irr, narcosis, liver damage, cardiac arrest
Forms carbon monoxide in blood and stresses heart suspect cancer agent	skin, URT, CNS, CVS	irr, narcosis, numbness, heart arrhythmias
One of least toxic	skin, CNS, heart	derm, narcosis, heart arrhythmias, dizziness
Do not use; suspect cancer agent; skin*	skin, CNS, resp sys, heart, liver, kidneys	irr, vertigo, visual disturbances, derm, nausea, heart arrhythmias
Do not use; suspect cancer agent; skin*	skin, CNS, liver URT, heart	irr, narcosis, heart arrhythmias, liver damage, flushing after alcohol consumption

continued

Table 8, *continued*

Common solvents and their hazards

Solvent class	TLV (ppm)	FP (°F)	VP (mm Hg)
Esters			
methyl acetate	200	14	173
ethyl acetate	400	24	76
isopropyl acetate	250	40	43
amyl acetate	100	77	4
Ethers			
Cellosolves (glycol ethers) & their acetates			
cellosolve (2-ethoxy ethanol, ethyl cellosolve, ethylene glycol mono-ethyl ether)	5	120	4
methyl cellosolve (ethylene glycol monomethyl ether, 2-methoxy ethanol)	5	107	6
butyl cellosolve (ethylene glycol) monobutyl ether, 2-butoxyethanol	25	141	0.6
Ketones			
acetone	750	1.4	266
methyl ethyl ketone (MEK)	200	21	70
methyl isobutyl ketone (MBK)	50	73	15
Others			
turpentine	100	95	5

Comments	Organs affected	Symptoms
Extremely flammable	eyes, skin, URT	irr, narcosis
Least toxic in class	eyes, skin, URT, CNS	irr, narcosis
	eyes, skin, URT, CNS	irr, narcosis
	eyes, skin, URT, CNS	irr, narcosis
Do not use; many form explosive peroxides with air; extremely flammable	eyes, skin, URT	irr, narcosis, derm
Try to avoid as a class		
skin*	skin, eyes, URT, CNS, kidney, liver, reproductive sys, blood	mild irr to skin, eyes, & URT, loss of appetite, narcosis, kidney failure
skin*	skin, eyes, URT, CNS, kidney, liver, reproductive sys, blood	irr, narcosis, renal failure, pulmonary edema, fatigue, anemia
skin*	skin, eyes, CNS, kidney, liver, lungs, blood, reproductive sys	irr, narcisos, renal failure, pulmonary edema, fatigue, anemia
least toxic in class; extremely flammable	skin, URT, CNS	irr, narcosis, derm
	skin, URT, CNS	irr, narcosis, derm
	skin, URT, CNS	irr, narcosis, derm
Use mineral spirits or odorless paint thinner when possible; skin*	skin, eyes, URT, lungs, CNS, kidney, bladder	irr, derm, narcosis, pulmonary edema, convulsions, kidney & bladder damage

Source: Reprinted in part from "Solvents in Museum Conservation Labs," (COH, 1985).

Plastics

Plastics—which have changed our lives greatly in the last few decades—have done some revolutionizing in theater as well. Theater workers use plastics as casting materials, glues, adhesives, structural elements, artificial snow, costume padding, textiles, and gels.

What is plastic?

A plastic or "polymer" is created when a chemical called a "monomer" reacts with itself to form long chains. This reaction is called polymerization. For example, when a monomer called methyl methacrylate is polymerized, it becomes *poly*methyl methacrylate, better known as Lucite or Plexiglas.

Some plastics are capable of a second reaction in which the long chains are linked together laterally (side by side). This reaction is called crosslinking. For example, liquid polyester resin becomes a solid material when it is reacted with a crosslinking agent like styrene.

These long-chain and crosslinked polymers possess different properties when exposed to heat. Heat usually will deform or mold long-chain polymers into new shapes. These polymers are called thermoplastics. On the other hand, heat will not deform crosslinked polymers, and these are called thermoset plastics.

Chemicals that can cause monomers and resin to react are given various names including actuators, curing agents, hardeners, crosslinking agents, or catalysts.

Hazards of plastic resin systems

Plastics are most hazardous during polymerization and crosslinking. Most monomers, initiators, and crosslinkers are very toxic. The hazards vary with each type of plastic resin system. Be sure you know which plastic you are polymerizing.

Polyester resins. Polyester casting systems (which are sometimes reinforced with fiberglass) are common in theater crafts. Hazardous chemicals used in casting include the crosslinking agent, which is usually styrene; ketone solvents, such as acetone, used to dilute the resin or for cleanup; the initiator, which is a peroxide, such as methyl ethyl ketone peroxide; and fiberglass.

Styrene is a highly toxic aromatic hydrocarbon solvent that can cause narcosis, respiratory system irritation, and liver and nerve damage. Acetone is a less toxic solvent, but is extremely flammable.

Methyl ethyl ketone peroxide can form an explosive mixture with acetone and has caused blindness when splashed in the eyes. Fiberglass dust can cause skin, eye, and respiratory irritation.

There are many other compounds in polyester resin systems that initiate, promote, or accelerate the reaction. For more complete information about these chemicals, consult the Center for Occupational Hazards' data sheet "Plastics Used in Theater Crafts."

Precautions for using polyester resins

1. Work only in areas that have a local exhaust system. Additional protection may be obtained by wearing a NIOSH-approved organic vapor respirator for solvent exposure, and add a dust filter if you use fiberglass.

2. Wear gloves and chemical splash goggles when handling and pouring materials. Protection from some plastic resin chemicals requires special types of gloves. Ask the manufacturer for advice.

3. Wear clothing that covers your arms and legs. Remove clothes immediately if they are splashed with resins or peroxides. Always remove clothing completely after work, then take a shower.

4. Cover exposed areas of your neck and face with a barrier cream as protection in case of splashes.

5. Handle peroxides correctly by following the advice in the section on organic peroxides. Be especially careful to avoid splashes in the eyes. Never mix peroxides with acetone.

6. Use acetone, not styrene, when you clean up. Cover your work area with disposable paper or towels to make cleaning easier.

7. Follow all precautions for using solvents, such as cleaning up spills immediately and disposing of rags in approved, self-closing waste cans.

8. When mixing small amounts of resins, use disposable containers and agitators such as paper cups and wooden sticks. If you need reusable containers, use polyethylene or stainless steel containers.

Silicone and natural rubber. Two types of silicone resin systems are used to make molds. The first is a single-component system that cures by absorbing atmospheric moisture. The second is a two-component system that cures by means of a peroxide. Both systems contain solvents such as acetone or methylene chloride.

Single-component systems release acetic acid or methanol into the air. Acetic acid vapors are highly irritating to the eyes and respiratory tract. Methanol is a nervous system poison. Two-component systems often contain chemicals that can damage the skin and sometimes also contain methylene chloride, which can cause narcosis and stress the heart.

You also can use water-based natural rubber latex to make molds. Some kinds of latex contain chemicals that can irritate the skin, but natural rubber is one of the safest molding systems to use. Rubber cement and some contact cements also contain natural rubber, but there are also very toxic solvents in these products. Many of these products contain n-hexane, which is especially toxic to the nervous system. When possible, select such products as Elmer's Rubber Cement, which uses the less toxic heptane as a solvent.

Precautions for using silicone and natural rubber

1. Use with sufficient ventilation to remove acetic acid, solvents, and other vapors.

2. Wear protective gloves. Consult the manufacturer of the resin or latex about the proper gloves to use.

3. If any components are liquid, wear goggles when you pour or handle them.

4. Follow all solvent precautions when you use products containing *any* solvents.

Epoxy systems. Epoxies are used for casting, laminating, and molding. They also are common adhesives and putties.

Epoxies are two-component systems. After the two are mixed, the resulting epoxy gives off heat, which vaporizes any solvents in it. An excess of hardener can cause the epoxy to heat to the point of decomposition and ignition.

Epoxy resins can irritate the skin. They also may contain varying amounts of solvents. Common solvents in epoxy include the glycidyl ethers, which have caused reproductive and blood diseases in animals, including atrophy of testicles, damage to bone marrow, and birth defects.

Epoxy hardeners are toxic and highly sensitizing to the skin and respiratory system. Almost 50 percent of workers regularly exposed to epoxy develop allergies to them.

Precautions for using epoxies

1. Wear goggles and gloves or barrier creams when you use large amounts of epoxy. Do not mold epoxy putties by hand unless you wear gloves; barrier creams do not provide sufficient protection.

2. When you use large amounts of epoxy, work either with local exhaust (such as a spray booth) or work in front of a window exhaust fan.

Polyurethane resins. Polyurethane resin systems usually consist of a polyol polymer resin (which might also contain metal salts or amine initiators) and isocyanate crosslinkers. Do not confuse these with polyurethane varnishes and paints, which are safer. Foam casting systems also contain blowing agents such as freon.

Theater crafts workers have used foam polyurethane casting in particular. Several shops have stopped using it because of its adverse health effects. Other theater shops should avoid these and other urethane systems for several reasons. First, the isocyanate crosslinkers (which are related to the chemical that caused over 2,000 deaths in Bhopal, India) are so irritating that, at very low levels, they can cause acute asthma-like respiratory distress and other symptoms. TLVs for the crosslinkers are so low that most theater shops cannot manage to achieve them. (The TLV for one common isocyanate—toluene diisocyanate—is 0.02 ppm.) NIOSH has not approved any air-purifying respirators for the crosslinkers. The final product, when heated or burned, can give off hydrogen cyanide, carbon monoxide, acrolein, and other toxic gases. And even cutting, sanding, and finishing the final product has been associated with skin and respiratory problems.

Precautions for using urethane resins

1. Do not allow anyone who has a history of allergies, heart problems, or respiratory difficulties to be exposed even peripherally to urethane resins.

2. Use them in a local exhaust system large enough to enclose the entire project. If you also need respiratory protection, use an *air-supplied* respirator with full face mask.

3. Wear protective clothing and gloves during foaming and casting.

4. Use ventilation while sanding and cutting finished plastic, and wear protective clothing and gloves.

Other resin systems. There are a number of other resin systems, but they are not used often in theater. However, systems employing methyl methacrylate (MMA) alone or in combination with other monomers are used occasionally. Some of these systems need special precautions because they involve elevated pressures, elevated temperatures, or both.

Investigate the hazards of plastic resin systems before using them in shops. Obtain MSDSs and other product information and be sure your shop is equipped with necessary ventilation.

Organic peroxides

Organic peroxides are used to initiate many polyester, acrylic, and even some silicone polymerizations. Do not confuse these with hydrogen peroxide, which is not very hazardous.

Hazards of organic peroxides. In general, organic peroxides burn vigorously and are both reactive and unstable. When old and decomposing, or when heated, some are shock-sensitive and can explode. Some can burn without air because they release their own oxygen. This makes it dangerous to mix them with flammable or combustible materials. For example, if peroxides ignite after being spilled on clothing, the fire cannot be put out with a fire blanket.

Because of organic peroxides' fire and explosion hazard, they usually are sold mixed with inhibitors. Even so, these mixtures have been known to burn quietly until all the inhibitor is burned off; then the fire intensifies.

The toxic hazards of organic peroxides are largely unknown. In general, their vapors may cause eye and respiratory irritation, and many are sensitizers.

Precautions for using peroxides

1. Obtain MSDSs and other information on peroxides. Pay special attention to information about reactivity, fire hazards, and spill procedures.

2. Store peroxides separately from each other and from other combustibles. Always keep peroxides in their original containers.

3. Do not store large amounts of peroxides or keep them for a long time. Dispose of supplies within the period of time specified on the label or MSDS (often six months or less).

4. Do not heat peroxides or store them in heat or sunlight.

5. Never dilute peroxides with other materials or add them to accelerators or solvents.

6. Wear protective goggles when pouring peroxides.

7. When mixing small amounts of resins and peroxides, use disposable containers. Soak all tools and containers in water before disposing of them.

8. Clean up spills immediately following MSDS directions. Inert materials such as unmilled fire clay usually are recommended to soak them up. Clean up peroxide-soaked material with non-sparking, non-metallic tools; do not sweep them because fires have started from the friction of sweeping itself.

9. If peroxide spills on your clothing, remove your clothes immediately and launder them well before wearing them again.

10. When discarding unused peroxide or fire clay/peroxide mixtures, mix them with a 10 percent sodium hydroxide solution. This will prevent fires because the reaction changes the peroxide into another, less flammable, compound.

Finished plastics

Rather than working with resin systems, it is easier and safer to work with sheets, films, beads, or blocks of finished plastic. Even so, when plastics are cut or heated, decomposition products are released and these products can be hazardous. Processes during which this can occur include sawing, sanding, hot knife or wire cutting, press molding, drilling, grinding, heat shrinking, vacuum forming, plastic burnout casting, torching, and melting. In general, the gases and smoke produced from the finished plastics during high-heat processes are usually more dangerous than those produced at lower temperatures.

Some plastics are especially hazardous to cut or heat. Among these are polyvinyl chloride (which produces hydrochloric acid gas) and all nitrogen-containing plastics, such as polyurethane, melamine resins, urea formaldehyde, and nylon. These latter produce hydrogen cyanide gas.

In addition, the dusts of some plastics are very sensitizing, and this dust will contain many potentially hazardous additives such as plasticizers (used to achieve the desired softness), stabilizers, colorants (dyes and pigments), fillers, fire retardants, inhibitors, accelerators, and more. Some of the common plasticizers (some of the phthalate esters) are known to cause cancer in animals. However, the vast majority of these additives' hazards are unknown.

Plastics adhesives also contain toxic solvents, which require their own precautions.

General precautions for working with finished plastics

1. Use good dilution ventilation or local exhaust ventilation. Use water-cooled or air-cooled tools, if possible, to keep decomposition to a minimum. When heat-forming plastics, use the lowest possible temperature.

2. Add a vacuum attachment to sanders, saws, and other electric tools to collect dust.

3. Select respiratory-protection equipment carefully. Air-purifying respirators worn when working with finished plastics may provide only partial protection from plastic decomposition products. A dust mask provides protection only against particles such as those produced by sanding or cutting plastics. An organic vapor respirator will trap some decomposition gases and vapors. An acid-gas-cartridge respirator will collect hydrochloric acid gas from decomposing polyvinyl chloride plastics. There are no approved cartridges for some gases and vapors; among this type are acrolein, hydrogen cyanide, isocyanates, and nitrogen oxides.

4. Clean up all dust carefully by wet mopping. Do not sweep.

5. Use the precautions for solvents when using plastics adhesives.

Woodworking

Wood is probably the most commonly used material in theater. Prop and scenery makers primarily use soft woods and plywood, but prop makers also may use old or exotic woods for furniture or other on-stage objects. Virtually any type of wood may end up in a shop, especially when "found" or used objects are collected and modified. This wide and unpredictable variety of woods means that theater wood-workers can encounter a wide variety of woodworking health hazards. A more detailed discussion of woodworking hazards can be found in the Center for Occu-pational Hazards' data sheet "Woodworking Hazards and Precautions."

Wood and sawdust hazards

Almost everyone who works with wood con-siders sawdust to be nothing more than a nui-sance. In fact, however, some wood dusts can cause allergies, some are toxic, and others contain toxic substances such as pesticides, preservatives, and silica. It has also been es-tablished that certain types of cancer are re-lated to wood-dust exposure.

Cancer. The most prevalent cancer related to wood dust is cancer of the nasal cavity and nasal sinuses. A recent twelve-country survey showed that an astonishing 61 percent of all such cancer cases occurred among woodworkers. Hardwood dusts are definitely implicated, but no studies have been conducted on workers exposed only to soft woods, so broader conclu-sions cannot be drawn.

The twelve-country survey also showed that 78.5 percent of a particular cancer, adenocarcinoma, occurred in woodworkers. Seven out of 10,000 wood-workers will develop adenocarcinoma each year, compared to only 6 out of 10 million annually in the general population. The average time from first exposure to onset of the cancer is forty to forty-five years and the cancer may develop even though decades may have passed during which the worker had no exposure to wood dust.

Most theater craft workers are exposed to much less dust than furniture workers, and they need not consider giving up wood as a stage material. But it is important to control wood dust. The American Conference of Governmental Hygienists recommends a TLV of 1 milligram per cubic meter (1 mg/m³) for hardwood dusts and 5 mg/m³ for soft-wood dusts.

Early symptoms of nasal sinus cancer may include persistent nasal dripping, stuffiness, or frequent nosebleeds. Such symptoms should be reported to a physician familiar with wood-dust hazards.

Dermatitis. Irritant dermatitis is one wood-related skin disease. Exposure to the sap and bark of some trees causes it, so it is only likely to affect theater workers if they cut trees, saw raw timber, or work with unusual woods such as cashew.

Sensitization dermatitis results from an allergy to certain sensitizing chemicals in some woods. Its symptoms may start as redness and irritation and may proceed to severe eczema, fissuring and cracking of the skin anywhere the body has been touched by the offending sawdust. The sensitizing chemicals are most likely to be found in many common hardwoods. Some exotic woods even have caused dermatitis in persons exposed only to the *solid* wood, not to its dust. Rosewoods are one such type. Prolonged contact with rosewood musical instruments, bracelets, or knife handles has been known to cause sensitization dermatitis.

Should you suspect that a skin problem is caused by a particular wood, a doctor can conduct a patch test on your skin. Should you need to identify an unusual wood, send a small piece of it (not sawdust) for testing to the US Department of Agriculture's Forest Products Research Laboratories in Madison, Wisconsin.

Respiratory system effects. Upper respiratory effects, such as damage to the mucous membranes, dryness and soreness of the throat, larynx, and trachea can be caused by some woods, especially sequoia and western red cedar. These effects may proceed to nosebleeds, coughing blood, nausea, and headache. Eye irritation usually occurs as well.

Lung problems—like asthma, alveolitis (inflammation of the lung's air sack)—affect a minority of workers exposed to irritant sawdusts. However, these are serious diseases and a few woods, such as sequoia and cork oak, can cause permanent lung damage. The symptoms may not appear until several hours after sawdust exposure, making diagnosis difficult. Any persistent or recurring lung problems should be reported to a physician familiar with wood-dust hazards.

Toxic Effects. Some woods contain small amounts of toxic chemicals that may be absorbed through the respiratory tract, intestines, or occasionally through skin abrasions. These chemicals may cause symptoms such as headache, salivation, thirst, nausea, giddiness, drowsiness, colic, cramps, and irregular heart beat. In

Table 9

Some woods and their health hazards

Commercial name(s)*	Family	Origin	Health effects
Maple	Aceraceae		D
Cashew	Anacardiaceae	America	D
Birch	Betulaceae		D
Gabon mahogany	Burseraceae	Africa	D, C-R, A, AL
Redwood	Caesalpinaceae	America	T
Virginian pencil cedar, Eastern red cedar	Cupressaceae	America, Asia	D, C-R, A, T
White cedar, western red cedar	Cupressaceae		D, C-R, A, T
White cypress pine	Cupressaceae	Oceania	D, C-R, A
Chestnut, beech, oak	Fagaceae		D, C-R, A
Walnut	Juglandaceae		D, C-R, A
American whitewood, tulip tree	Magnoliaceae	America	D
Red cedar, Australian cedar	Meliaceae	America, Asia	D, C-R, A
Mahogany, Honduras mahogany, American mahogany, baywood	Meliaceae	America	D, C-R, A, AL, T
White handlewood	Moraceae	Oceania	D, T
Alpine ash, yellow gum, mountain ash	Myrtaceae	Oceania	D, C-R, A
Ash	Oleaceae		D
Ebony, rosewood, blackwood, jacaranda, foxwood	Papilionaceae	Africa, Asia, America	D, C-R, A, T
Pine, silver fir, European larch, Douglas fir, red fir, Douglas spruce	Pinaceae		D, C-R, A
European spruce, whitewood, black spruce	Pinaceae	Asia	D, C-R, A, AL
New Zealand white pine	Podocarpaceae	Oceania	D, C-R, A
Cherry, black cherry	Rosaceae		D, C-R, A
Boxwood	Rutaceae	America	D, C-R, A
Poplar	Salicaceae		D, C-R, A
Sequoia, California redwood	Taxodiaceae	America	D, C-R, A, T

* Different commercial names are sometimes given to different species within the same family. For example, oak, chestnut, and beech are in the same family and have the same health effects, but redwood and California redwood are not in the same family; white cypress pine, pine, and New Zealand pine are also not in the same family. To identify a wood's hazards, its exact species, and origin may be required. Woods can be identified by the Forest Products Research Laboratory, Madison, Wisconsin, a branch of the US Department of Agriculture.

Key to Health Effects
D   Dermatitis
C-R Conjunctivitis-rhinitis
A   Asthma
AL   Allergic Asthma
T   Toxic effects

Source: International Labor Organization, Encyclopedia of Occupational Health and Safety, 3d ed. (Geneva, 1983).

exceptional cases, poisoning has occurred from food containers, spoons, or spits made from woods such as yew or oleander.

Should you suspect that your symptoms are related to a particular wood, inform a physician and have the wood identified.

Hazards of wood additives and preservatives

Almost every wood you use has been treated in some way with additives, pesticides, preservatives, or all three. These chemicals can vary from relatively safe additives to highly toxic pesticides. Until recently it was virtually impossible to find out exactly what chemicals had been used on woods.

Three of the most common types of wood preservatives—pentachlorophenol (PCP) and its salts, arsenic-containing compounds, and creosote—have been re-classified by the Environmental Protection Agency as "Restricted Use Pesticides." Now warnings will accompany wood treated with these chemicals, and over-the-counter wood stains and preservatives will not contain them.

These three types of preservatives are associated with cancer, birth defects, and other hazards. Theater workers should discard old wood products containing them and avoid wood treated with them. There are many other more suitable preservatives on the market.

Precautions with wood and sawdust

1. Try to purchase wood from suppliers who know where the wood they sell comes from and how it was treated, and who are well informed in general about their products.

2. Avoid wood treated with PCP, arsenic, or creosote.

3. Equip all woodworking machinery with local exhaust dust collection systems. Ideally, these systems should vent to the outside rather than return air to the shop.

4. Wear a NIOSH-approved dust mask when dust cannot be controlled easily, such as during hand sanding.

5. Wear protective clothing to keep dust off your skin. Wear gloves or barrier creams when handling woods known to be strong sensitizers.

6. Practice good hygiene. Wash and shower often. Keep the shop clean.

Solvent-containing products

Many finishes, adhesives, paints, and paint removers contain solvents. All solvents are toxic and most are flammable.

Glues and adhesives

Many skin conditions and allergies can be caused by wood glues and adhesives. Epoxies, for example, can cause blistering, allergic dermatitis, and asthma. Adverse reactions to epoxy are seen in almost 50 percent of all workers who use it regularly.

Urea-formaldehyde and phenol-formaldehyde resins and glues release formaldehyde gas, a strong eye and respiratory irritant and allergen. For more detailed information, see the Center for Occupational Hazards' data sheet "Formaldehyde."

Glues and cements that contain solvents can dry and de-fat the skin, making it more subject to infections. You are also likely to inhale toxic solvent vapors.

Polyvinyl acetate (PVA) emulsion glues, such as Elmer's, are much safer than other types of wood glue. These glues require longer setting times than some of the solvent adhesives and epoxies, but you should use them whenever you can.

Safe use of more hazardous adhesives requires avoiding skin contact, sparing and careful use, keeping containers closed as much as possible during application, and good general shop ventilation.

Vibrating tools

Almost every theater worker has experienced a tingling in his or her hands or arms after using vibrating tools such as orbital sanders or power saws. In most cases the tingling disappears within an hour. However, a significant number of people are at risk from a more permanent condition known as "white hand," "dead fingers," or Raynaud's syndrome. This disease, more correctly called Vibration Syndrome, progresses in stages. First there is intermittent tingling and numbness, even when tools have not been used. Then fingertips are seen to blanch, especially in cold weather. Finally, fingers blanch extensively, well beyond the tips, in both hot and cold weather. Much pain, and ulcerated and gangrenous fingers, occur in such cases.

A 1983 NIOSH comprehensive study concluded that vibrating tools can cause advanced stages of this disease in as little as one year of regular hand-tool use. NIOSH recommends redesigning tools; being alert to symptoms; keeping them in good condition; taking ten-minute work breaks after every hour of continuous exposure; maintaining normal and stable workplace temperatures (especially avoiding cold temperatures); and not grasping the tool harder than needed for safe use (tight gripping of the hands increases the likelihood of damage).

Noise

Noise levels are measured in decibels (dB) on a logarithmic scale. Every increase of 10 dB means a tenfold increase in noise intensity. For example, ordinary conversation averages about 60 dB, while the average circular saw produces between 100 and 109 dB. Saws, planers, routers, sanders, and the like can easily produce a cacophony of ear-damaging sound waves.

The longer you are exposed to excessive noise, the greater the damage to your ear. This fact is reflected in the OSHA standard for noise, which restricts louder sounds to shorter periods of time. For example, the Permissible Exposure Limit (PEL) for an eight-hour day is set at 90 dB, whereas noise at a level of 110 dB is restricted to periods of time less than one-half hour.

Measuring precise noise levels takes skill and special equipment not usually available in theater shops. However, you may assume that you need ear protection if you must talk loudly to be heard one or two feet away, if you have ringing in your ears, or if you experience difficulty in hearing after work.

Prevention of hearing damage begins with the machines that make the noise. Try to purchase well engineered, quiet machines. You can also buy dampering equipment, such as mufflers and other sound-absorbing materials, with some machines. All machines run more quietly when they are well oiled and carefully maintained. If you mount machinery on a rubber base, you will reduce vibration transmission and rattling.

If noise levels are still high in your shop, wear ear protection. For light noise, special and readily available ear plugs can suffice (do not improvise with cotton or other materials). For heavy noise exposure, use the protectors that look like ear muffs. A physician should evaluate people who have already lost some hearing before they are exposed to noise that may cause further impairment.

Machine guards

OSHA standards require guards on saws and other pieces of woodworking equipment. Machines in theater shops, however, are commonly found unguarded. Their accident potential is obvious, and both home and industrial shop statistics document that such accidents occur frequently.

People may find guarded saws awkward the first time. But workers accustom themselves quickly to guards on saws (and other machines), and soon will not want to work without them.

Fire hazards

The National Fire Protection Association reports that scores of fires and explosions occur annually in woodworking shops. One reason is that fine wood dust in a confined area can explode with tremendous force if ignited with a spark or match. Combining wood dust, machinery, and flammable solvents greatly increases the hazard.

Fire prevention authorities agree that adequate ventilation is the best way to curb the risk of fire. Ventilation should be combined with safe solvent handling, good housekeeping, and regular removal of dust and scraps.

Medical surveillance for woodworkers

1. Know the symptoms and diseases your woods can cause. When possible, avoid toxic or allergy-provoking woods.

2. Be able to give your doctor a good occupational history. Know the chemicals to which you are exposed by getting MSDSs on the products you use. Keep records of exposures and symptoms.

3. Remember, if a health problem lessens on weekends or during vacations, it may be related to your work.

4. Have your physician pay special attention to your sinuses and upper respiratory tract. Report symptoms like nasal dripping, stuffiness, or nosebleeds.

5. Have your physician include a pulmonary function test in your regular physical examination every two or three years to detect lung problems early.

6. Have a base line hearing test and periodic hearing tests as often as your doctor suggests.

7. Be prepared for accidents: know your blood type, wear an alert tag if you have special medical problems, and keep up with your tetanus shots.

8. Should symptoms or illness occur and persist even after treatment, seek the advice of a specialist, such as a doctor who is board certified in occupational medicine.

Asbestos

Media coverage of actor Steve McQueen's battle with cancer and his subsequent death may have made a strong impression, but it is highly likely that many people quickly forgot the nature of the cancer that killed him—mesothelioma. Many may have forgotten, too, that mesothelioma is almost invariably caused by asbestos exposure.

The source of the asbestos that triggered Steve McQueen's illness is not known with certainty. One press account blamed asbestos clothing and padding that he used for fire protection when he was a race driver. As an actor, however, he could have been in contact with the many sources of asbestos used in theater work. For example, there are many old, damaged asbestos theater curtains; asbestos-insulated wiring on lighting instruments; deteriorating asbestos soundproofing or insulation; asbestos soldering blocks and boards; vermiculite dusts; dusts from asbestos-coated welding and brazing rods; instant papier-mâchés; mixtures of glue and powdered asbestos fibers formerly used for texturing scenery; and even asbestos flakes used to imitate falling snow. Who in theater work has not come into contact with one or more of these?

Although the amount of asbestos from some of these sources may be small, it is still sufficient to cause asbestos-related diseases. Recently the NIOSH-OSHA Asbestos Work Group reviewed asbestos studies and concluded that there is no level of asbestos exposure below which there are no clinical effects. Exposure duration studies suggest that exposures as brief as one day to three months can bring on significant disease.

Dramatic evidence of this can be seen in the asbestos-related diseases suffered by members of asbestos workers' households or by persons who have lived near asbestos-contaminated areas. These household and community contacts involve low-level or intermittent, casual exposure, such as dust brought home on a worker's clothing.

These studies make it obvious that the release of even small amounts of asbestos fibers should be considered hazardous. Once asbestos fibers are airborne, they will persist. They are virtually indestructible and invisible. They are also more buoyant than ordinary dust. They can be stirred up on the slightest air currents and can float almost indefinitely where they can be inhaled easily. So even occasional or sporadic release of asbestos fibers produces a buildup of airborne asbestos, meaning continuous exposure to all persons in the area.

Asbestos-related diseases

Inhaled asbestos is known to cause three diseases: asbestosis, ordinary lung cancer, and mesothelioma (a cancer of the lining of the chest and abdomen). Asbestos also has been linked to other malignancies, such as stomach and intestinal cancer.

Asbestosis is a lung-scarring disease caused when a considerable amount of asbestos dust is inhaled. On the other hand, very small amounts of asbestos may cause lung cancer and mesothelioma, although the chances of getting either increases as the exposure to asbestos increases.

Asbestos insulation

Asbestos insulation of ceilings and pipes is a particular popular concern. Between 1940 and 1973, hundreds of thousands of tons of asbestos were sprayed on or applied to ceilings and other parts of many theaters, schools, and other public and private buildings. Surveys indicate that 5 to 15 percent of the nation's public schools contain some asbestos materials. Once these products deteriorate and release fibers—the term is "become friable"—they can be considered very hazardous. In some schools, levels of asbestos in the air have exceeded the federal safety standards for asbestos workers.

In 1973, the Environmental Protection Agency prohibited the spraying of asbestos materials for fireproofing and insulation. As of June 28, 1983, the EPA required all public and private elementary and secondary schools in the country to survey and identify all asbestos materials applied to structural surfaces. If friable asbestos-containing materials were found, the school administrators were to inform employees and parent-teacher groups.

Theaters in elementary and secondary schools, therefore, already should have been surveyed for friable asbestos. Theaters that are not in schools, however, have not been required to make these surveys. Wisdom and prudence dictate undertaking surveys, even if the regulations do not apply to your theater.

Remove, isolate, or encapsulate? When friable asbestos is found, a decision must be made about whether to remove it, to isolate it, or to encapsulate it.

Removing asbestos is costly and hazardous. Under no circumstances should theater workers attempt to remove even the smallest amounts of it themselves. Instead, the work should be done by workers specially trained to do the job in accordance with all appropriate OSHA and EPA regulations including isolating the work area with plastic barriers and negative pressure, handling the material only when it is wet, wearing protective clothing and respiratory protection, cleaning up with specially filtered (HEPA) vacuum cleaners, and repeatedly testing the air to monitor any escape of asbestos fibers into the workplace.

In some cases, asbestos can be left intact sealed behind air-tight barriers, such as specially lowered ceilings. This solution is not usually preferred, because later damage to the ceiling or having to reach wiring or pipes behind the barrier may mean exposing the asbestos.

Another method of containing asbestos is to encapsulate it. Specially trained workers apply a special sealant that penetrates the asbestos insulation and hardens to hold it in place. Encapsulation usually is much cheaper than removal, and it at least partially preserves asbestos' insulating and fireproofing attributes. How long the encapsulant will remain intact, however, is a matter for conjecture.

The EPA has been evaluating the various sealants already on the market. Information about the ones that have proved effective can be obtained from Julius Brodsky, Asbestos Technical Advisor, US-EPA, Region II, Room 1015, 26 Federal Plaza, New York, NY 10278.

Asbestos substitutes

Theater workers can choose among fiberglass or synthetic mineral fiber substitutes for almost all of the asbestos-containing products they use. However, some people worry that even these man-made fibers may turn out to be hazardous.

Studies of fiberglass workers to date show only an increase in non-malignant lung diseases such as chronic bronchitis. Animal studies also indicate that if glass and mineral fibers are spun to diameters thicker than natural asbestos, they do not provoke cancer. Still, caution should be exercised when using fiberglass and mineral fibers.

Non-asbestos products

A number of major companies now manufacture mineral and glass fibers that are processed into textiles (useful for theater or welding curtains), construction boards, and insulation. Many products made of these substitute materials are advertised in theater and safety supply catalogs. For less common or special items, you may wish to seek advice from one of the earliest mineral fiber manufacturers: Carborundum Corporation, Insulation Division, Box 808, Niagara Falls, NY 14302. Best's Safety Directory also contains sources for many non-asbestos products.

Theater curtains. Most large theater catalogs list sources of non-asbestos theater curtains. One such source is W.E. Palmer Company, 134 Southampton Street, Boston, MA 02118.

If replacement is not economically feasible, be sure that the asbestos curtain is painted to keep fibers from becoming airborne.

Gloves. Old and worn asbestos gloves have long been known to release dangerous amounts of fibers. A study done by the NIOSH-OSHA Asbestos Work Group has shown that even brand-new gloves also release substantial amounts of fiber into workers' breathing zones under conditions of normal use.

Sources of non-asbestos gloves can be found in most safety supply catalogs, such as *Best's Safety Directory.*

Insulated wire. Almost every theater in the country has many lighting instruments that are wired with asbestos-coated wires. It would be economically difficult to discard these instruments and more difficult to rewire the lamps safely. The worker doing the rewiring would be working with asbestos and should take all the precautions asbestos workers do.

Some lighting technicians have resorted to slipping teflon sleeves or shields over the exposed parts of the wire and taping the ends. This provides a kind of encapsulation. Teflon tubing can be purchased in many lighting supply stores. Someday, we hope a company is established that will rewire instruments at a price small theaters can afford.

Other asbestos-insulated wires, such as twofers, can be replaced with teflon-coated wire.

Other asbestos products

Theater workers and teachers should discard supplies of old papier-mâché, asbestos-coated welding rods (these are no longer made and good replacements exist), and any other suspect materials. Testing these products to see if they contain asbestos is more expensive than replacing them.

Vermiculite mined in the United States is also asbestos-contaminated (the dust may contain 3 to 5 percent asbestos). Unless you are sure the vermiculite is African in origin, discard it.

Theatrical makeup

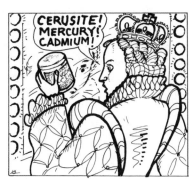

Today, acutely toxic chemicals like lead and mercury rarely are found in cosmetics. Modern laws in many countries demand that chemicals proposed for addition to cosmetics first undergo testing for acute toxicity. Nevertheless, significant numbers of consumers still suffer ill effects from cosmetics. In addition, studies show that beauticians and cosmetologists (who are exposed to more cosmetics than average members of the population) suffer a higher incidence than average of lung problems like asthma and chronic bronchitis, more skin rashes, and more frequent kidney and liver damage. Studies also show that they have a higher incidence of cancer and reproductive problems like toxemia of pregnancy and miscarriages.

No similar studies have been made of actors and makeup artists, who are exposed regularly to theatrical cosmetics, but there are numerous documented incidents of makeup affecting individual actors adversely. One well-known example is Buddy Ebsen's serious reaction to silver makeup, which cost him the role of the Tin Man in *The Wizard of Oz*.

A more detailed discussion of makeup hazards and precautions can be found in the Center for Occupational Hazards' data sheet "Makeup and Cosmetic Aerosol Sprays."

How makeup causes harm

In order to harm you, makeup must enter your body; all three of the entry routes are possible.

Skin contact with some makeup chemicals can cause skin problems such as irritation, infection, and allergic reactions. Some makeup chemicals also can penetrate the skin and enter the blood stream.

95

Inhalation of powders and aerosol sprays is another way makeup and cosmetic chemicals can enter your body. Studies have shown that inhalation of aerosol sprays can damage or destroy the tiny hair-like cilia that sweep foreign particles from the lungs. When the lung's defenses are weakened in this way, inhaled substances can cause even more damage.

Ingestion of lipsticks, wetting brushes with the mouth, and eating, smoking, or drinking while applying makeup will put the substances directly into your digestive tract.

Skin diseases

The most common reaction to cosmetics is an infectious reaction of the skin. Especially common is a condition known as "acne cosmetica," or cosmetic acne. Its acne-like skin eruptions affect about one-third of adult American women, and one prominent expert has stated that these eruptions usually are caused by facial cosmetics. (Cosmetic acne should not be confused with "acne vulgaris," which is associated with the onset of puberty.) Cosmetic acne usually is a mild condition. Small pimples appear and disappear intermittently and affect women from their twenties through their fifties.

Other types of skin and eye infections can result from cosmetics that support bacterial growth or that irritate the skin.

Irritant dermatitis. Chemicals that are caustic, acid, or strong oxidizers can harm the skin by attacking its surface. Examples include sodium and potassium hydroxides that can be found in cuticle softeners and hair relaxers. An example of a strong oxidizer is peroxide, which is used to lighten facial hair.

Organic solvents such as alcohol and acetone also can irritate the skin. Solvents can remove natural oils, leaving the skin cracked and dry.

Skin cancer. Sunlight is the major cause of skin cancer, but some chemicals have been shown to cause it, too. One example is carbon black, which was common in mascara until it was banned for cosmetics by the US Food and Drug Administration.

Allergic (contact) dermatitis. Many people develop allergies to chemicals in cosmetics. Estimates are that one person in ten is allergic to one or more fragrances in cosmetics. Some of the preservatives used in makeup also cause allergic responses.

Chrome and nickel compounds have been known to cause severe allergies and skin ulcers in industrial workers exposed to them. Chrome compounds can be found in some eye cosmetics, especially in blue and green hues. Nickel allergy has been documented in hairdressers.

Eye diseases

The skin around the eyes is more sensitive and more easily penetrated than facial skin. All types of skin diseases (infection, irritation, allergic dermatitis, and cancer) that affect facial skin also can affect the skin around the eyes. The membrane covering the eye and lining the eyelids (the conjunctiva) can be affected by cosmetic chemicals, producing inflammation (conjunctivitis).

Scratching the eyeball during application of eye makeup is the most common eye injury related to cosmetics. Nationwide health data from 1977 show that of the 2,739 persons who received emergency room treatment for cosmetic-related eye injuries, 2,413 were associated with mascara. Most of these were injuries to the eye surface.

Once an eye abrasion has occurred, the possibility of infection increases. These infections are infrequent, but some have caused ulcers on the cornea, have caused lashes to fall out, or, rarely, have caused blindness.

Cosmetic chemicals

Both theater and consumer makeups contain essentially the same ingredients. The differences between them stem from the fact that theater makeups are intended for use under harsh lights. They will have more yellow or orange pigments; they may have a stronger covering power at the expense of a more natural look; and their matching face powders are neutral or translucent so they will not change the base color. These differences are minor, and many professional actors include consumer makeup products in their kits.

Learning about the chemicals in makeup is easier now that manufacturers of consumer cosmetics have been required by law to list ingredients on product labels. An exception to complete ingredient labeling is occasionally granted by the FDA to certain manufacturers who claim that their particular ingredients are trade secrets. These products can be identified when the phrase "and other ingredients" is included on the label. Experts recommend avoiding these products.

Many theatrical makeup manufacturers also list their ingredients on product labels, although they are not required to do so. Use only these labeled products, because labeling helps to identify which ingredients are causing symptoms; to protect the consumer from paying high prices for inferior ingredients; and to choose products with ingredients best suited for the intended theatrical effect.

Although the lists of ingredients on makeup containers may seem long and complex at first, dedicated label readers soon will see that makeup ingredients fall into a few basic categories. There are minerals such as talc, kaolin, chalk, zinc oxide, and titanium dioxide; vegetable or organic powders such as corn or rice flours or starch; a host of oils and waxes such as vegetable oils and mineral (petroleum-derived) oils; dyes and pigments; and preservatives and fragrances.

Dyes and pigments are easy to identify on labels because their names are assigned by the FDA. These names indicate whether they are approved for food, drugs, and cosmetics (for example, FD&C Yellow No. 5) or only for drugs and cosmetics (for example, D&C Red No. 7). These names are different from Color Index names and numbers.

Basic classes of makeup

There are five basic types of makeup: face powders, rouges, foundation creams, mascaras, and lipsticks. In addition, there are various specialty makeups such as face putty, latex, and waxes.

Powders. Almost no reports of serious skin or eye infections from face powders are found in medical literature. Most powder ingredients are inert minerals such as talc, chalk, or kaolin; they are unlikely to cause skin reactions. Allergic responses to powders usually can be traced to perfumes, preservatives, or binding agents added to the powders. Bismuth oxychloride added for a metallic or pearl lustre has pro-duced photosensitivity (skin reactions provoked by sunlight) in some people. Get-ting powder into the eyes has caused conjunctivitis, but such powder-related in-flammations usually are temporary.

In the past, some cosmetic talcs contained asbestos. Now a voluntary industry standard prohibits manufacturers from using asbestos-contaminated talc in cosme-tics. You should suspect old face powders and talcum powders of containing asbestos and discard them.

Rouge. Rouge, whether in powder form or compact form, has the same ingredients as face powders, plus some added coloring. Cream rouges are made of coloring agents suspended in either oils and fat or in emulsions of water and oils.

No cases are found in the medical literature of serious infections due to rouge, but emulsion-based rouges are known to worsen dermatological problems. The detergents in emulsion rouges also enable dye particles to penetrate both hair follicles and cracks in the skin, resulting in irritation.

Foundation makeups. Foundation makeups have the same formulas as liquid rouge, except that they have more face powder and less pigment. Solid makeups are simply a cream base plus face powder.

Some physicians blame foundation face creams and makeups for cosmetic acne. Some animal studies indicate that many ingredients in these creams are slightly to moderately acnegenic.

Lipsticks. These are made basically of oily liquids, waxes, and pigments. Other ingredients may be fruit flavors and perfumes.

Lipsticks are associated with a special form of dermatitis called cheilitis. It is a drying or cracking of the lips, and usually is caused by eosin dyes, which stain the lips. Commonly used eosin dyes are D&C reds No. 21 and No. 27, and D&C Orange No. 5. Experts recommend avoiding these staining lipsticks. Lanolin and perfumes also may cause cheilitis.

Cancer-causing dyes were used in lipsticks in the past, so you should avoid using old cosmetics. Two dyes used currently (D&C reds No. 9 and No. 19) are thought to be possible carcinogens, and D&C Orange No. 5 has been approved only provisionally. To be on the safe side, you may want to avoid these dyes.

Mascara. An assortment of pigments, fats, and waxes is common to all mascaras. Cream mascaras are created when these ingredients are emulsified with water; solid mascaras, when they are suspended in soap; liquid mascaras, when they are dissolved in alcohol. All forms contain preservatives to inhibit bacterial growth.

Table 10

Acnegenic ingredients found in cosmetics

Ingredient	Acnegenicity
Butyl stearate	Moderate to strong
Cocoa butter	Strong
Corn oil	Weak to moderate
Isopropyl-myristate	Weak
Lauryl alcohol	Weak
Linseed oil	Strong
Margarine	Weak
Methyl oleate	Weak to moderate
Mineral oil	Varies from non-acnegenic to moderately acnegenic
Oleic acid	Strong
Olive oil	Moderate to strong
Peanut oil	Moderate to strong
Petroleum	Varies from non-acnegenic to moderately acnegenic
Safflower oil	Weak
Sesame oil	Moderate to strong
Stearic acid	Weak

Source: Tom Conry; David and Nan Fry; Allen Okagaki, *Consumer's Guide to Cosmetics* (New York: Doubleday, 1980).

Although some people react allergically to mascara ingredients, the major problem is that they can be contaminated with bacteria that can lead to conjunctivitis or eye infection. Both time and frequency of use will affect the rate at which bacteria grow in mascara. For this reason, you should discard old mascara. Using saliva to moisten brushes adds to the contamination.

The most common problem from using mascara is injury to the eye surface from the applicator. Infections following such an injury are not frequent, but they can be serious. You should seek treatment if you sustain this kind of injury.

Special makeups. Putty, wax, beeswax, and morticians' wax all can be used to build up a part of the face for theatrical purposes. They all have similar properties, but they differ slightly in hardness. Collodion can be used to create mock wrinkles or scars. Latex can be made to function in many of these ways, and it also acts as a glue, as does spirit gum.

Many people respond allergically to these products. One well-known makeup artist told of a case of spirit-gum allergy severe enough to require hospital treatment. Another makeup expert avoided an actor's allergy to spirit gum by placing surgical adhesive tape on his face before applying the spirit gum. Collodion allergies also are well known. People who are allergic to one of these products usually can find another that will work just as well.

You can replace spirit gum with surgical adhesive when resistance to moisture and excessive motion of the skin are not called for. Surgical adhesive was developed for medical purposes and is far less damaging to the skin. It is commonly used to fasten false eyelashes to eyelids and can be purchased in most drug and cosmetic stores.

It can be harmful to remove spirit gum and latexes by pulling them off the skin. Removing them with acetone or alcohol can dry or crack the skin. Instead, peel them off gently and use as little solvent as possible. Once they are removed, use oil, emollients, or moisturizers as needed to counter drying effects.

Nail products. Nail polishes, when used properly, are probably reasonably safe because the amount of solvent that can be inhaled when they dry is very small, and because the fingernail itself is probably the toughest, most chemically resistant area of the body. Some women have developed dermatitis when nail polish has contacted their skin. Inhalation of nail polish vapors has been reported to cause symptoms of nausea.

Polish removers, on the other hand, consist primarily of acetone, a solvent that can be a fire hazard and cause narcosis when significant amounts are inhaled. Although serious poisonings are rare, inhalation of acetone and other polish remover solvents can cause headache, fatigue, and bronchial irritation.

Of greatest concern are the new liquid nail products that dry and harden to create long false nails. Some of these contain plastic acrylate monomers, formaldehyde, and other highly sensitizing and toxic chemicals. Be sure to apply these only in very well ventilated areas and to avoid exposure to skin and broken skin. Should symptoms occur, discontinue use immediately.

When skin trouble strikes

When skin problems arise, consult a dermatologist, who can tell you which type of dermatitis you have and how to treat it. In general, if your problem is diagnosed as irritant dermatitis or cosmetic acne, you should identify the offending cosmetic and not use it again until healing is complete. The best permanent solution would be to stop using cosmetics altogether. Since this is not possible if you are a working actor, you can begin to try makeups, lotions, and moisturizers that do not contain acnegenic or irritating chemicals. In addition, keeping your skin free of makeup except when absolutely necessary will help.

Table 11

Ingredients to avoid in lotions and moisturizers
Isopropyl myristate. Penetrates skin readily, can cause irritation.
Propylene glycol. Can cause allergic and toxic reactions.
SD alcohol. Dries the skin.
Urea. Reacts with protein (skin) and can cause irritation.
Ethylene glycol. Can form toxic oxalic acid.
Quaternium-15 and formaldehyde. These preservatives have track records for irritation.
DEA, TEA. May indicate the presence of carcinogens;
2-bromo-2-nitropropane-1,3-diol. May indicate the presence of carcinogens; forms formaldehyde.

Source: "Cosmetic Science, a 1975 Literature Survey," in *Cosmetics and Toiletries*, Vol. 91 (April, 1976), 25–36.

If the doctor decides you are allergic to some cosmetic ingredient, you have a more serious problem on your hands. However, there are several steps you can take. Try hypoallergenic makeup. The term hypoallergenic has no legal meaning, and no government standard applies to such makeups. However, reputable manufacturers honestly try to eliminate those ingredients known to produce allergies in many people.

Try unscented makeups or products with a wholly different scent. One person in ten has an allergy to fragrances and you may be one of them. Or try a makeup with a different preservative. Preservatives are known to cause allergic dermatitis in some people. Three preservatives recognized as especially hyperallergenic are quaternium 15, imidazol idinyl urea, and parabens (both methyl and propyl parabens). Look for them on the label.

Try comparing labels of products to which you respond, looking for ingredients they have in common. Some likely candidates for causing allergies are cocoa butter, FD&C Red No. 11, Vitamin E, the eosin dyes in lipsticks, and chrome compounds.

General rules for using cosmetics

1. Use only cosmetic products on your skin. Never use paints, dyes, or other non-cosmetic substances.

2. Purchase only ingredient-labeled cosmetics. Many good professional theatrical brands of makeup are now labeled.

3. Wash your hands before and after applying makeup. Makeup artists should wash their hands before they start on each client, and they should wash or discard sponges and brushes after using them on each client.

4. Never lend your makeup to anyone, and never borrow or accept used makeup from anyone.

5. Do not use aerosols and do not smoke in small, poorly ventilated dressing rooms.

6. Replace old cosmetics regularly. Do not buy cosmetics that look old or shopworn.

7. Avoid creating clouds of face powder or talcum powder that can be inhaled. Discard old face and bath powders.

8. Moisten brushes or pencils with clean tap water, not with saliva.

9. Seek medical advice about, and treatment for, eye injuries, dermatitis, acne, and other skin and eye conditions.

10. Avoid smoking, eating, or drinking when applying makeup.

11. When removing spirit gum, latex, and the like, avoid prolonged skin contact with solvents such as acetone; replace lost skin oils and moisture.

Fog, smoke, and other effects

Everyone who watches movies, television commercials, and videos of all sorts has seen how rapidly the use of special effects such as smoke, fog, and pyrotechnics has increased. Sometimes these effects have been involved in accidents ranging in seriousness from Michael Jackson's slicked hair catching fire to the deaths of actor Vic Morrow and two young children during the filming of *The Twilight Zone*. In addition to such obvious accidents, there may be danger from hidden health effects owing to exposure to some smokes and fogs.

Today's theater, too, uses more special effects. Smoke, fog, fireworks, gun shots, flash pots, and the like commonly are used in productions from Broadway to public schools all over the continent. Regrettably, these effects often are used without proper precautions and without permission from authorities who have jurisdiction over their use. The selection and use of special theatrical effects deserves far more thought and care.

Fog and smoke toxicity

For over forty years, various compounds and mixtures have been vaporized, sprayed, and burned to create fog, smoke, haze, and mist on theater stages and movie sets. Recently new products for this purpose have been developed and added to the theater's bag of tricks. Recently, too, the Center for Occupational Hazards has received many inquiries about the safety of these products, and more and more complaints of physical symptoms from some people exposed to them.

In order to meet this growing demand for information, COH has been attempting to collect Material Safety Data Sheets (MSDSs) and other ingredient information about various smokes and fogs. Our efforts have been only partially successful because some companies do not respond to written inquiries; some companies respond but refuse to send MSDSs; some send MSDSs containing little or no ingredient information (claiming the ingredients are trade secrets); and some send only product literature that routinely makes unsubstantiated claims of nontoxicity.

However limited the information may be, you should keep in mind certain principles when you evaluate manufacturers' claims. Smoke and fog, for example, are *inhaled*, so you should consider predominantly a product's toxicity by this route of entry. For example, mineral oil is of very low toxicity when ingested, but when inhaled it can cause pulmonary edema and other lung problems. Be sure to ask manufacturers of nontoxic products how they have tested them.

Keep in mind that acute toxicity testing of fogs and smokes provides no information about products' long-term effects.

Liquid and solid fog and smoke products may change chemically when they are fumed or misted. You should know a product's toxicity when it is in its final form.

Minor health effects that are not reported in tests with animals could be very important in theater. Rats, for example, cannot tell scientists that a substance gives them sore or dry throats. Yet a sore or dry throat could be a serious problem for a singer or actor. The Center for Occupational Hazards has received many complaints about throat irritation from people exposed to some fogs.

Consider exposure of high-risk individuals such as children and people with lung or heart disorders. The label on one product, for example, warns that people with asthma should not be heavily exposed to it, yet no one screens actors and audiences medically prior to such exposure. In general, never expose high-risk individuals to fogs and smokes that have known adverse effects, that have OSHA PELs, or whose effects are unknown.

Manufacturers of smoke and fog often assume that actors, stage hands, and technicians are exposed to safe amounts of these products because they are used only on well-ventilated stages for short periods of time. However, concentrations of mists and smoke thick enough to see can contain large amounts of chemicals (possibly in excess of industrial short-term limits for some chemicals), and in many cases, people do work in poorly ventilated situations for long periods of time. In addition, many stages are not equipped with ventilation capable of keeping smoke and fog from reaching audiences. Audiences have a right to expect to watch a show without assuming any risk at all from special effects.

Fog and smoke safety hazards

Some smokes and fogs are fire and safety hazards. Some organic chemical mists are flammable, combustible, or explosive in the presence of sparks, flames, or hot lights. Petroleum distillates, for example, are capable of causing a fire or of exploding under the right conditions. Check product labels and MSDSs for a product's flash point and other fire and explosion data. If the product is flammable or combustible, ask the manufacturer if the product's flammability has been tested in mist form.

Some fog products leave a greasy, slippery residue on walking surfaces, and the residue can cause accidents. Heavy fog effects can also obscure an actor's vision, allowing accidents to happen.

Types of fog and smoke

In general, fog and smoke products create their effects by vaporizing or misting organic chemicals such as petroleum distillates; by misting mixtures of water and organic chemicals such as glycerine and glycols; by subliming dry ice; by heating or fuming inorganic chemicals such as ammonium, zinc, or titanium chlorides; or by burning organic materials such as gums, paper, and resins.

Organic chemical fogs. Misting organic chemicals from specially designed machines or from aerosol spray cans or other pressurized devices are probably the most popular fogging technique.

Organic chemical fogs that contain petroleum distillates are the most hazardous, and should be avoided. Petroleum distillates are either flammable or combustible, and in mist or aerosol form they can be explosive. In addition, moderate exposure to petroleum distillate mists can cause eye, throat, and lung irritation. Heavy exposures can cause pulmonary edema. Petroleum distillates are also narcotic and damaging to the central nervous system.

Fogs created by misting other organic chemicals (such as high molecular weight oils) will have other hazards. Each chemical should be identified and researched before subjecting actors and other personnel to it.

Water/organic chemical fogs. The substantial amount of water in these products virtually eliminates their fire hazards, and it reduces but does not eliminate their potential health hazards. The organic chemicals in some of these products include glycerine, glycols such as ethylene, diethylene, and propylene glycol, and triols. Glycerine has no significant hazards if ingested, but it is a respiratory irritant. Propylene glycol has been known to cause allergic and toxic reactions when applied to the skin. The inhalation hazards of propylene glycol, diethylene glycol, and many of the other chemicals are largely unknown because so little testing has been done.

Dry ice fogs. The safest fogs employ dry ice. These fogs are carbon-dioxide-rich mists from subliming dry ice, and can be hazardous only if they are used so heavily that they would replace oxygen necessary for breathing.

Dry ice fog has aesthetic disadvantages, however, because the mist is cold and tends to layer near the floor and dissipate quickly. Methods of generating dry ice fogs at heights above the stage so they disperse as they fall improve the effects somewhat.

Chloride-containing smokes. All chloride-containing smokes are irritating to the lungs. Sal ammoniac (ammonium chloride), one of the most common, is the least irritating, but it still can cause respiratory problems when used in large amounts or around high-risk people. Zinc chloride, a component of some common theatrical smoke products, is a stronger irritant and in the lungs can produce hydrochloric acid. Titanium tetrachloride is so irritating that products containing it should not be used at all in theater.

Most of these products were developed originally to study airflow patterns, ventilation systems, etc. They were never intended for theatrical purposes and their MSDSs contain strong warnings about inhaling the smoke. One manufacturer's MSDS recommends that users employ self-contained breathing apparatus under conditions of heavy exposure.

Smoke from burning gums, resins, etc. Smoke from the combustion of any organic material (gums, resins, paper, wood, and the like) contains a combination of toxic and irritating substances. Although some smokes are more hazardous than others (such as highly toxic smoke from burning plastics), all smokes are harmful at high doses. Olebanum (frankincense) and perfumed or spice-containing products produce pleasant-smelling smokes but they too are harmful. Persons with respiratory problems or allergies especially should shun smokes.

Rules for using fog and smoke products

1. Purchase only products for which you have ingredient lists or good MSDSs. Be sure the information you have describes the hazards of the smoke or fog itself and not merely the starting ingredients, if they are altered by burning or misting. The Center for Occupational Hazards has information on common fog and smoke products that you can obtain on request.

2. Consider the limitations of the theater or facility before electing to use fog or smoke. For example, if the ventilation system is not capable of keeping chemicals from reaching the audience, use only dry ice.

3. Select the safest product for the job. If children, elderly, or high-risk individuals will be exposed, do not use products with hazardous ingredients or products containing ingredients whose hazards are unknown.

4. Plan to use fog or smoke in low, safe concentrations. Avoid billowing, thick effects that could endanger actors' health and safety.

5. Hold a meeting with all personnel who may be exposed to the fog or smoke before you use it so you can inform them about the potential hazards. The meeting should be designed to consider individual health problems and to pool everyone's knowledge about possible safety hazards, such as obscured vision or slippery floors. If there are children in the cast, invite their parents to the meeting.

6. Set up lines of communication for health or safety complaints should there be adverse reactions or problems after the material is in use.

Other effects

Use of firearms, flash pots, open flames (such as real fireplaces and flaming torches), or any kind of fireworks all may come under the control of a theater's local fire department. Before using any of these techniques, consult the local fire marshal or fire department. Allow enough lead time to meet local requirements before your production opens.

You usually must obtain waivers in order to use these pyrotechnical devices legally. Some of these processes can be carried out only by a licensed pyrotechnician. Obtaining this license from the fire department usually involves passing a special test. In some locations the use of firearms also requires waivers from the local police department.

Pyrotechnical displays, laser shows, and other dangerous special effects should be contracted to specialists who already have the required expertise and licenses.

Welding

All types of welding can be extremely hazardous. Nowhere in theater shops is there a greater potential for fires, burns, electrical hazards, explosions, and health hazards than from welding.

All methods of welding or cutting metal rely upon heat—either from burning gas or from an electric arc—to do the job. Over eighty different types of welding exist and use these basic heat sources in various ways. But in theater, the types most commonly used are oxyacetylene welding, ordinary arc welding, gas metal arc welding (metal inert gas, MIG), and gas tungsten arc welding (tungsten inert gas, TIG).

Basic rules and regulations

Safe welding requires knowledge, training, and compliance with health and safety codes and regulations. Welders and those responsible for administering or setting up theater welding shops should be thoroughly familiar with the American National Standards Institute's Standard A49.I, "Safety in Welding and Cutting"; the National Fire Protection Association NFPA codes; the OSHA General Industry Standards; and all other state and local codes applying to welding operations. These codes and standards will guide you in planning and maintaining a safe shop.

At least one welder in your shop should have professional training in the kind of welding you are doing. For example, the American Welding Society (AWS) considers I25 to I50 hours of professional training necessary to qualify for oxyacetylene, oxyfuel gas welding, brazing, and flame cutting (they are taught as a unit). Another 250 to 300 hours' training are required to qualify for arc welding.

Welders who teach students or supervise other welders should have additional training in health and safety. This training can be obtained by attending health and safety seminars conducted by the AWS or the National Safety Council.

Busy shops, where welding is frequent or continuous, should be prepared to comply with the OSHA standards for welding fumes and gases. Careful assessment of the ventilation and the welding materials, and frequent air sampling may be necessary to ensure that the standards are not violated.

Unfortunately, most theater shops do not meet these basic welding safety and health requirements. Theater craftspeople, especially in small theaters and schools, commonly pick up welding by trial and error and by observing other—usually unqualified—welders. In addition, they often weld with old, poorly maintained equipment. Their workspace is usually unventilated and located near activities or materials that can interact dangerously with the welding process. For example, one university theater shop carried on welding near an open elevator shaft. Welding sparks actually started fires in oily residue at the shaft's bottom five or six times before the university relocated this operation.

Welding safety

Welding safety is an extraordinarily complex subject, and the safety rules differ depending on the type of welding, the kind of work, and on the shop or on-site conditions. These rules should be gleaned from accepted standards, codes, and regulations. Certain general rules, however, are basic to common types of welding used in theater.

Good housekeeping. Keep welding shops scrupulously organized and clean; nothing extraneous should be stored in it. Eliminate combustible materials from the area to the extent possible. Make sure nothing is on the floor that welders can trip over. A welder's vision is often limited by face shields or goggles.

Electrical safety. Most shocks caused by welding equipment are not severe, but they still can cause injury or even death. Involuntary muscle contractions from mild shocks can lead to accidents, and the heart can stop if moderate amounts of current are directed across the chest. Avoid these hazards by using only welding equipment meeting national standards, such as those of the National Electrical Manufacturers' Association. Follow all equipment operating instructions to the letter. Keep clothes dry (even from excessive perspiration) and do not work in wet conditions. And be sure to inspect all electrical connections, cables, and electrode holders before you start to weld.

Compressed gas cylinder safety. Compressed gas cylinders are potential rockets or bombs. If mishandled, cylinders, valves, or regulators can break or rupture, causing damage as far as 100 yards away.

The different kinds of gases inside the cylinders are themselves hazards. There are three basic types of hazardous gases. *Oxygen* will not burn by itself, but ordinary combusible materials like wood, cloth, or plastics will burn violently or even explode when ignited in the presence of oxygen. *Fuel gases,* such as acetylene, propane, and butane, are flammable and can burn and explode.

Shielding gases are used to shield processes such as MIG and TIG welding and include argon, carbon dioxide, helium, and nitrogen. They are inert, colorless, and tasteless. If they build up in confined spaces, such as in your enclosed welding area, they will replace air and can asphyxiate people in the area.

Many regulations and standards protect welders from the hazards of compressed gas cylinders. Whether they weld or not, all theater technicians should be familiar with some basic rules.

Only cylinders approved for use in interstate commerce should be accepted. Do not remove or change the numbers or marks stamped on cylinders, but when you return empty cylinders to the vendor, mark them "EMPTY" or "MT" with chalk. Close the valves and replace valve protection caps. Do not tamper with safety devices in valves.

Cylinders too large to carry easily may be rolled on their bottom edges, but never dragged. Protect cylinders from cuts, abrasions, falls, or from striking each other. Never use cylinders as rollers, supports, or for any purpose other than that intended by the manufacturer. Always treat cylinders with the same care you would if they were full, even if they are not. Accidents have resulted when containers under partial pressure have been mishandled.

Secure cylinders by chaining, tying, or binding them, and always use them in an upright position. Store the cylinders in cool, well-ventilated areas or outdoors in vertical positions (unless the manufacturer suggests otherwise). The temperature of a cylinder should never exceed 130°F. Do not store oxygen cylinders near fuel cylinders or combustible materials.

Fire safety. Over 4 percent of all industrial fires are started by welding sparks. What we call sparks are actually molten globules of metal that can travel up to forty feet and still be hot enough to ignite combustible materials. Welding shops must be free from cracks or crevices into which sparks may fall and smolder. No combustible material should be allowed in the shop.

Fire extinguishers must be on hand in welding shops because other methods—such as overhead sprinkler systems—can be dangerous. Each welder should be given formal instruction about using the shop's extinguishers.

On-site welding in locations other than the shop (such as on or near the stage) is necessary in some theaters. It requires extra precautions, and formal policies for on-site welding should be developed for such theaters. Some sensible rules include: Advance notice must be given before welding; all other activities in the area must be curtailed; all combustibles within forty feet of the operation must be removed or a special fireproof curtain and covering must be installed to shield combustibles that cannot be removed; floors should be cleared and dampened; and a fire watcher should be at the ready with an extinguisher during the welding operation. As in industry, the fire watcher should remain for half an hour after welding has been completed.

Health hazards

The health hazards of welding are less obvious than the safety hazards of welding. Health hazards vary among different types of welding, and include: radiation, heat, noise, fumes and gases from welding processes, and gases from compressed cylinders.

Radiation. There are three forms generated by welding. *Visible* light is the least hazardous and most noticeable radiation emitted by welding. Intense light produces only temporary visual impairment, but protect your eyes from strong light.

Infrared (IR) radiation is produced when matter is heated until it glows—as during welding, cutting, brazing, or soldering operations. IR can cause temporary eye irritation and discomfort. Repeated exposures can cause permanent eye damage, including retinal damage and infrared cataract. Chronic IR eye damage of these types occurs slowly and without warning.

Ultraviolet (UV) is the most dangerous of the three types of radiation. All forms of arc welding produce UV radiation. Eye damage from UV, often called a "flash burn," can be caused by less than a minute's exposure. Symptoms usually do not appear until several hours after exposure. Severe burns become extremely painful, and permanent damage may result.

UV also can damage exposed skin. Chronic exposure can result in dry, brown, wrinkled skin, and may progress to a hardening of the skin called keratosis. Further exposure is associated with benign and malignant skin tumors.

Heat. Welders can be burned by heat from IR radiation or from hot metal. "Heat stress" can result if body temperature is raised to hazardous levels.

Noise. A welder's hearing can be damaged by the noise. Fortunately, most welding processes used in theater produce noise at levels below the OSHA PELs; air carbon arc cutting is one of the possible exceptions. If you wear ear plugs, make sure they are fire resistant. Several cases of eardrum damage have been reported when an overhead spark fell into an ear canal that was either unprotected or contained a combustible plug.

Fumes and gases. These are produced during the welding process and sometimes are seen as a smoky plume rising from the weld. Fumes are created whenever metal is melted, just as water gets into the air when it evaporates. Once this metal vapor is released, it reacts with air to form tiny metal oxide particles called fumes.

Welding gases can come from gas cylinders or can be created when substances burn during welding. Gases can form when some types of welding rods are being used, or when coated metals are welded.

Table 12

Common airborne contaminants from welding coated metals

Coating	Contaminant(s)
Paint	Chromium, lead, mercury, zinc, copper, cadmium, etc.
Galvanizing	Zinc oxide
Metal spray	Copper, chromium, nickel, aluminum, zinc
Plating	Cadmium, chromium, nickel, copper
Degreasing or cleaning solvents	Phosgene, hydrochloric acid

Table 13

Contaminants created from welding, cutting, and allied processes

Fumes	Gases
Aluminum	Ethylene
Copper	Phosphine
Iron	
Manganese	*Asphyxiant*
Magnesium	Acetylene
Molybdium	Argon
Tin	Carbon dioxide
Zinc	Helium
	Nitrogen
Known or suspect carcinogen	Propane
Beryllium	
Cadmium	
Chromium	*Highly toxic or irritating*
Nickel	Carbon monoxide
	Chlorides
Highly toxic	Fluorides
Fluorides	Oxides of nitrogen
Lead	Phosgene
Vanadium	Sulphur dioxide

Many occupational illnesses are associated with substances found in welding fumes and gases, including metal fume fever (with symptoms similar to flu), and a variety of chronic lung diseases including chronic bronchitis. Lung and respiratory system cancer are associated with metal fumes such as chrome, nickel, beryllium, and cadmium.

Precautions

Isolate the welding area. Isolation keeps other workers from being exposed either to direct or reflected radiation. Walls, ceilings, and other exposed surfaces should have dull finishes from special nonreflective paints. Portable, fire-resistant, UV-impervious screens or curtains can be purchased to isolate welding areas and to separate individual welding stations.

Use eye protection such as goggles or face shields. Each welder needs individual protection for the type of welding he or she does. Welders who use methods that leave a slag coating on the weld should wear safety glasses under their shields. Too often injury occurs when welders raise their hoods to inspect a weld and the slag pops off unexpectedly.

Face and eye protection equipment should be cleaned carefully after each use and inspected routinely for damage, especially for light shield damage. A scratched lens will permit radiation to penetrate, and it should be replaced.

Visitors and other workers nearby should avoid looking at welding and should wear safety glasses (UV weakened by distance is stopped by glass).

Wear protective clothing. The rest of a worker's body needs to be defended as well. Pants and long-sleeved shirts can protect legs and arms. Many welders prefer wool fabrics that insulate them from temperature changes and because they emit a strong odor when heated or burned. Treat cotton clothing with a flame retardant. Never wear polyester or synthetic fabrics; they melt and adhere to the skin when they burn. Pants and shirts should not have pockets, cuffs, or folds into which sparks may fall.

Wear gloves when arc welding. Shoes should not have openings into which sparks can fall. Hair should be covered, or at least tied back. Leather aprons, leggings, spats, and arm shields may be needed for some types of welding. Do not use asbestos protective clothing.

Use good ventilation. Welders need to be protected from gases, fumes, and heat buildup. Equip shops with local exhaust ventilation systems, such as downdraft tables or flexible duct fume exhausters, to capture welding fumes and gases at their source. Such ventilation is especially necessary in theater because welders often work with metals whose composition is unknown, presenting unknown hazards.

These local exhaust systems should be combined with dilution systems to reduce heat buildup and to remove gases and fumes that escape collection. A simple exhaust fan may suffice for open-area welding, while enclosed MIG and TIG welding booths will need floor-level dilution systems to prevent layering of inert gases.

Do not rely on respiratory protection; it is much less effective than ventilation. No single air-purifying respirator will protect you against all the contaminants in welding fumes. Metal-fume filters will stop fumes, but they offer no protection from gaseous contaminants. Some air-supplied respirators can provide welders with fresh air, but these are complex pieces of equipment effective only when maintained properly and only when their users have had proper training. They are usually not practical for theater use.

Table 14

Filter lens shades

Welding operation	Shade no.
Shielded metal-arc welding: 1/16-, 3/32-, 1/8-, 5/32-inch electrodes	10
Gas-shielded arc welding (nonferrous): 1/16-, 3/32-, 1/8-, 5/32-inch electrodes	11
Gas-shielded arc welding (ferrous): 1/16-, 3/32-, 1/8-, 5/32-inch electrodes	12
Shielded metal-arc welding: 3/16-, 7/32-, 1/4-inch electrodes	12
5/16-, 3/8-inch electrodes	14
Atomic hydrogen welding	10–14
Carbon arc welding	14
Soldering	2
Torch brazing	3 or 4
Light cutting, up to 1 inch	3 or 4
Medium cutting, 1 inch to 6 inches	4 or 5
Heavy cutting, 6 inches and over	5 or 6
Gas welding (light) up to 1/8 inch	4 or 5
Gas welding (medium) 1/8 inch to 1/2 inch	5 or 6
Gas welding (heavy) 1/2 inch and over	6 or 8

Note: In gas welding or oxygen cutting where the torch produces a high yellow light, it is desirable to use a filter or lens that absorbs the yellow or sodium line in the visible light of the operation.

Source: ANSI Z87.1-1979.

Table 15

Selection chart for eye and face protectors

Selection Chart for Eye and Face Protectors for Use in Industry, Schools, and Colleges

This Selection Chart offers general recommendations only. Final selection of eye and face protective devices is the responsibility of management and safety specialists. (For laser protection, refer to American National Standard for Safe Use of Lasers, ANSI Z136.1-1976.)

1. GOGGLES, Flexible Fitting, Regular Ventilation
2. GOGGLES, Flexible Fitting, Hooded Ventilation
3. GOGGLES, Cushioned Fitting, Rigid Body
*4. SPECTACLES, without Sideshields
5. SPECTACLES, Eyecup Type Sideshields
6. SPECTACLES, Semi-/Flat-Fold Sideshields
**7. WELDING GOGGLES, Eyecup Type, Tinted Lenses (Illustrated)

7A. CHIPPING GOGGLES, Eyecup Type, Clear Safety Lenses (Not Illustrated)
**8. WELDING GOGGLES, Coverspec Type, Tinted Lenses (Illustrated)
8A. CHIPPING GOGGLES, Coverspec Type, Clear Safety Lenses (Not Illustrated)
**9. WELDING GOGGLES, Coverspec Type, Tinted Plate Lens
10. FACE SHIELD, Plastic or Mesh Window (see caution note)
* 11. WELDING HELMET

*Non-sideshield spectacles are available for limited hazard use requiring only frontal protection.
**See Table A1, "Selection of Shade Numbers for Welding Filters," in Section A2 of the Appendix.

APPLICATIONS		
OPERATION	**HAZARDS**	**PROTECTORS**
ACETYLENE—BURNING ACETYLENE—CUTTING ACETYLENE—WELDING	SPARKS, HARMFUL RAYS, MOLTEN METAL, FLYING PARTICLES	7, 8, 9
CHEMICAL HANDLING	SPLASH, ACID BURNS, FUMES	2 (For severe exposure add 10)
CHIPPING	FLYING PARTICLES	1, 3, 4, 5, 6, 7A, 8A
ELECTRIC (ARC) WELDING	SPARKS, INTENSE RAYS, MOLTEN METAL	11 (In combination with 4, 5, 6, in tinted lenses, advisable)
FURNACE OPERATIONS	GLARE, HEAT, MOLTEN METAL	7, 8, 9 (For severe exposure add 10)
GRINDING—LIGHT	FLYING PARTICLES	1, 3, 5, 6 (For severe exposure add 10)
GRINDING—HEAVY	FLYING PARTICLES	1, 3, 7A, 8A (For severe exposure add 10)
LABORATORY	CHEMICAL SPLASH, GLASS BREAKAGE	2 (10 when in combination with 5, 6)
MACHINING	FLYING PARTICLES	1, 3, 5, 6 (For severe exposure add 10)
MOLTEN METALS	HEAT, GLARE, SPARKS, SPLASH	7, 8 (10 in combination with 5, 6, in tinted lenses)
SPOT WELDING	FLYING PARTICLES, SPARKS	1, 3, 4, 5, 6 (Tinted lenses advisable; for severe exposure add 10)

CAUTION:
• Face shields alone do not provide adequate protection.
• Plastic lenses are advised for protection against molten metal splash.
• Contact lenses, of themselves, do not provide eye protection in the industrial sense and shall not be worn in a hazardous environment without appropriate covering safety eyewear.

Source: ANSI Z87.1–1979.

Table 16

Summary of general precautions for welders

Radiation (UV, IR, light). Wear proper goggles and/or face shield for the type of welding. Do not wear contact lenses. Cover skin with gloves and clothing, preferably made of wool.

Heat. Provide sufficient dilution ventilation to cool the room and remove some fumes (minimum ventilation of 2000 cubic feet per minute per welder, per ANSI Z49.1.8.2.2).

Welding plume, fumes, and gases. Have local exhaust ventilation such as flexible duct, bench slot hood, or downdraft table. Respiratory protection may be used under some conditions.

Inert shielding gases or fuel gases. Local exhaust ventilation is preferred. For welding booths, provide openings at floor level to prevent gas buildup. Do not use air-purifying respirators.

Sparks, hot metal, slag pop-offs, etc. Wear safety glasses, flame-resistant clothing and gauntlet gloves, leather or flame-resistant aprons, leggings, and high boots for heavy work. Wear skull caps and shoulder covers for overhead work, and ear protection to stop sparks.

Noise. Wear flame-resistant ear plugs or muffs. Do not wear headphones.

Welding heavy objects. Wear safety shoes and safety hats.

Appendix

Where to get help

ACTS (Arts, Crafts and Theater Safety)
181 Thompson Street, #23
New York, NY 10012   (212) 777-0062
Contact person: Monona Rossol

The Center for Occupational Hazards (COH)
5 Beekman Street
New York, NY 10038   (212) 227-6220
Contact person: Christine Proctor

Northwestern Medical Program for Performing Artists
Northwestern Memorial Hospital
Superior and Fairbanks Court
Chicago, IL 60611   (312) 902-ARTS
Contact person: Alice G. Brandfonbrenner, M.D.

Catherine and Gilbert Miller Health Care Institute for Performing Artists
St. Luke's-Roosevelt Hospital
425 West 59 Street, 6th floor
New York, NY 10019   (212) 554-6314
Contact person: Emil Pascarelli, M.D.

The National Institute for Occupational Safety and Health (NIOSH)
Robert A. Taft Laboratories
4676 Columbia Parkway
Cincinnati, OH 45226

NIOSH can answer inquiries about health and safety, investigate hazardous work-sites, and distribute publications. The ten NIOSH regional offices referred to in the text have been closed due to funding cuts.

The National Fire Protection Association (NFPA)
Batterymarch Park
Quincy, MA 02269   (617) 770-3000

The NFPA answers inquiries about fire, safety, rescue, and electrical hazards; sets standards; and publishes codes. Of special interest to theater workers is the National Electrical Code.

The National Safety Council (NSC)
444 North Michigan Avenue
Chicago, IL 60611   (312) 527-4800

The NSC has access to information and statistics on safety and publishes newsletters—such as the "Campus Safety Newsletter"—for specific target groups. They also teach courses on health and safety, including a welding safety and health course.

The American Welding Society (AWS)
PO Box 351040
555 NW LeJeune Road
Miami, FL 33135   (305) 443-9353

The AWS has technical information on welding and teaches courses on welding safety.

Bibliography

A wide variety of data sheets about art hazards are available from the Center for Occupational Hazards. Send a self-addressed, stamped envelope to The Center for Occupational Hazards, 5 Beekman Street, New York, NY 10038; upon request, we will also send a publications list and a complimentary copy of the *Art Hazards News*.

*Recommended supplementary data sheets

Air-Purifying Respirators for Theater Crafts
Bibliography
Children's Art Supplies Can Be Toxic
Dye Hazards and Precautions
Theatrical Fog and Smoke
Fiber Art Hazards and Precautions
Formaldehyde
Introduction to Theater Hazards
Labels: Understanding and Using Them
Paints Used in Theater Crafts
Plastics Used in Theater Crafts
Reproductive Hazards in the Arts and Crafts
Solvents Used in Theater Crafts
Theatrical Makeup and Cosmetic Aerosol Sprays
Ventilation for Theater Crafts
Woodworking Hazards and Precautions

Recommended periodicals

*Art Hazards News. Center for Occupational Hazards, New York. 10 issues a year.
Theater Crafts. Theater Crafts, PO Box 630, Holmes, PA 19043. 10 issues a year.

Selected theater references

American Theatre Planning Board, Inc. *Theater Check List*. Middletown, CT: Wesleyan University Press, 1969.

Association of Theatrical Artists and Craftspeople. *The New York Theatrical Sourcebook*. New York, 1984 (updated yearly).

Baker, Hendrik. *Stage Management and Theatercraft*, 3d ed. London: J. Garnet Miller, 1981.

Bellman, Willard F. *Lighting the Stage*. New York: Chandler Publishing Co., 1974.

Calvert, Don. *Theater Safety*. New York: US Institute of Theater Technology (work in progress).

Conry, Tom, and the Science Action Coalition. *Consumer's Guide to Cosmetics*. New York: Anchor Books, 1980. Out of print.

Gillette, A. S. and J. M. *Stage Scenery Construction and Rigging*, 3d ed. New York: Harper and Row, 1981.

Gillette, J. Michael. *Designing with Light: An Introduction to Stage Lighting*. Palo Alto, CA: Mayfield Publishing Co., 1977.

Illuminating Engineering Society. *I.E.S. Handbook*. New York, 1981.

Parker, W. Oren and Smith, Harvey K. *Scene Design and Stage Lighting*, 4th ed. New York: Holt, Rinehart & Winston, 1979.

Pook, Barbara. *Rigging Components and Application*. New York: Drama Book Publishers, 1985.

*Rossol, Monona. "Papier-Mâché Hazards." *The Puppetry Journal*, vol. 3, no. 1, 1981.

Stern, Lawrence. *Stage Management: A Guide to Practical Techniques*. Boston: Allyn & Bacon, 1974.

Texas Education Agency. *Guidelines for Theater Safety*. Austin: TEA, 1981.

Tompkins, Dorothy Lee. *Handbook for Theatrical Apprentices*. London: Samuel French, 1962.

Welker, David. *Stage Craft: A Handbook for Organization, Construction and Management*. Boston: Allyn & Bacon, 1977.

General References on Health and Safety

A. M. Best Company. *Best's Safety Directory*, 2 vols. Oldwick, NJ: A. M. Best, 1985 (updated yearly).

American Conference of Governmental Industrial Hygienists. *Documentation of the Threshold Limit Values*, 4th ed. Cincinnati: ACGIH, 1980 (updated regularly).

*Available from the Center for Occupational Hazards.

————. *Threshold Limit Values for Chemical Substances and Physical Agents in the Work Environment.* Cincinnati: ACGIH, 1984 (updated yearly).

*American Mutual Assurance Alliance. *Handbook of Organic Industrial Solvents,* 5th ed. Chicago: AMAA, 1980.

American National Standards Institute. *Practice for Occupational and Educational Eye and Face Protection,* ANSI Z87.1-1979. New York: ANSI, 1980.

————. *Safety in Welding and Cutting,* ANSI Z49.1-1973. New York: ANSI, 1973.

American Welding Society. *Fumes and Gases in the Welding Environment.* Miami: AWS, 1979.

————. *The Welding Environment.* Miami: AWS, 1973.

"Air Cleaners." *Consumer Reports,* January 1985.

*Committee on Industrial Ventilation. *Industrial Ventilation: A Manual of Practice,* 19th ed. East Lansing, MI: ACGIH, 1985 (updated yearly).

Firenze, Robert B. and Walters, James B. *Safety and Health for Industrial/Vocational Education for Supervisors and Instructors.* Washington, D.C.: NIOSH/OSHA, 1981.

Gosselin, Robert, Roger Smith and Harold Hodge. *Clinical Toxicology of Commercial Products,* 5th ed. Baltimore: Williams and Wilkins, 1984.

Hamilton, Alice and Hardy, Harriet. *Industrial Toxicology,* 3d ed. Acton, MA: Publishing Sciences Group, 1974.

Hawley, Gessner, ed. *The Condensed Chemical Dictionary,* 10th ed. New York: Van Nostrand-Reinhold, 1981.

International Labor Office. *Encyclopedia of Occupational Safety and Health,* 3d ed., 2 vols. Geneva: ILO, 1983.

National Fire Protection Association. *National Electrical Code Handbook,* 3d ed., Quincy, MA: NFPA, 1983 (updated regularly).
NFPA #30, *Flammable and Combustible Liquids Code.*
NFPA #10, *Portable Extinguishers.*
NFPA #494L, *State Fireworks Law.*
NFPA #51, *Welding and Cutting.*
NFPA #70, *National Electrical Code.*
NFPA #102, *Assembly Seating, Tents, Air-Supported Structures.*
NFPA #1123, *Fireworks, Public Display.*

National Institute for Occupational Safety and Health. *A Guide to Industrial Respiratory Protection,* DHEW (NIOSH) #76-189. Washington, D.C.: GPO, 1976.

————. *NIOSH Certified Equipment List As of September 1, 1983,* DHEW (NIOSH) #83-122. Washington, D.C.: GPO, 1980 (updated regularly).

*Available from the Center for Occupational Hazards.

———. *Occupational Diseases: A Guide to Their Recognition*, revised ed. Washington, D.C.: GPO, 1977.

———. *Occupational Safety and Health in Vocational Education*. DHEW (NIOSH) #79-138. Washington, D.C.: GPO, 1979.

———. *Occupational Safety and Health Program Guidelines for Colleges and Universities*, DHEW (NIOSH) #79-108. Washington, D.C.: GPO, 1978.

———. *The Industrial Environment: Its Evaluation and Control*. Washington, D.C.: GPO, 1973.

———. *NIOSH Registry of Toxic Effects of Chemical Substances (RTECS)*, 3 vols., DHEW (NIOSH) PB 85-218071. Springfield, VA: National Technical Information Service, 1981-2.

———. *RTECS 1983 Supplement*, DHEW (NIOSH). Washington, DC.: GPO, 1983.

National Safety Council. *Accident Prevention Manual for Industrial Operations*, 8th ed. Chicago: NSC, 1981.

Patty, Frank, ed. *Industrial Hygiene and Toxicology*, 3d ed., vol. II, 3 parts. New York: Interscience Publishers, 1982.

Power Tool Institute. *Power Tool "Safety Is Specific."* Brochure No. 585. Rolling Meadows, Illinois: P.T.I., 1984.

Sax, N. Irving. *Dangerous Properties of Industrial Materials*, 5th ed. New York: Van Nostrand-Reinhold, 1979 (updated regularly).

Stellman, Jeanne and Daum, Susan. *Work Is Dangerous to Your Health*. New York: Vintage, 1973.

Strong, Merle, ed. *Accident Prevention Manual for Training Programs*, revised ed. American Technical Society, 1975.

US Consumer Products Safety Commission. *Federal Hazardous Substances Act Regulations*. *Federal Register*, September 27, 1973.

US Department of Health, Education, and Welfare.
   Respiratory Protection: A Guide for the Employee, DHEW (NIOSH) # 78-193B. Washington, D.C.: GPO, 1978, reprinted 1979.

   Respiratory Protection: An Employer's Manual, DHEW (NIOSH) # 78-193A. Washington, D.C.: GPO, 1978.

US Department of Labor. *General Industry Occupational Safety and Health Standards*, 29CFR 1910. *Federal Register*, June 1981 (updated regularly).

Art Hazards References

American Society for Testing and Materials. *Standard Practice for Labeling Art Supplies for Chronic Health Hazards*, ASTM D4236. Philadelphia: ASTM, 1983.

*Available from the Center for Occupational Hazards.

Carnow, Bertram. *Health Hazards in the Arts and Crafts*. Chicago: Hazards in the Arts, 1975.

Challis, Tim and Gary Roberts. *Caution: A Guide to Safe Practice in the Arts and Crafts*. Sunderland, England: Sunderland Polytechnic Faculty of Art and Design, 1984.

*Clark, Nancy, Thomas Cutter and Jean-Ann McGrane. *Ventilation: A Practical Guide*. New York: Center for Occupational Hazards, 1984.

Eastman Kodak Co. *Safe Handling of Photographic Chemicals*. Rochester: Eastman Kodak, 1979.

Jacobsen, Lauren. *Children's Art Hazards*. New York: Natural Resources Defense Council, 1984.

*Jenkins, Catherine. "Textile Dyes Are Potential Hazards." *Journal of Environmental Health*, March/April 1978, 18.

*McCann, Michael. *Artist Beware: The Hazards and Precautions in Working with Art and Craft Materials*. New York: Watson-Guptill, 1979.

*McCann, Michael. "The Impact of Hazards in Art of Female Workers." *Preventive Medicine*, September 1978.

*McCann, Michael and Monona Rossol. "Health Hazards in the Arts and Crafts." Unpublished paper presented at 1981 American Chemical Society Annual Meeting, New York, August 25, 1981.

Miller, Barry, Aaron Blair and Michael McCann. "Mortality Patterns Among Professional Artists: A Preliminary Report." *Journal of Environmental Pathology, Toxicology and Oncology*, 1985 (in press).

Moses, Cherie, James Purdham, Dwight Bowbay, and Roland Hosein. *Health and Safety in Printmaking: A Manual for Printmakers*. Edmonton: Occupational Hygiene Branch, Alberta Labor, 1978. Out of print.

Ontario Crafts Council. *Crafts and Hazards to Health Bibliography*. Toronto: Ontario Crafts Council, 1980.

*Rickard, Ted and Ronald Angus. *A Personal Risk Assessment for Craftsmen and Artists*. Ontario Crafts Council and College, University and School Safety Council of Ontario, Toronto: 1983.

*Rossol, Monona. "Teaching Art to High Risk Groups." Center for Occupational Hazards data sheet.

*Available from the Center for Occupational Hazards.

Index

Allworth Press publishes quality books for artists, authors, graphic designers, illustrators, photographers, and small businesses. Titles published to date include:

The Artist's Complete Health and Safety Guide
by Monona Rossol (328 pages, 6 X 9", $16.95)

Business and Legal Forms for Authors and Self-Publishers
by Tad Crawford (176 pages, 8 7/8 X 11", $15.95)

Business and Legal Forms for Fine Artists
by Tad Crawford (128 pages, 8 7/8 X 11", $12.95)

Business and Legal Forms for Graphic Designers
by Tad Crawford and Eva Doman Bruck (208 pages, 8 7/8 X 11", $19.95)

Business and Legal Forms for Illustrators
by Tad Crawford (160 pages, 8 7/8 X 11", $15.95)

Business and Legal Forms for Photographers
by Tad Crawford (192 pages, 8 1/2 X 11", $18.95)

Caring for Your Art by Jill Snyder (176 pages, 6 X 9", $14.95)

The Graphic Designer's Basic Guide to the MacIntosh
by Michael Meyerowitz and Sam Sanchez (144 pages, 8 X 10", $19.95)

How to Sell Your Photographs and Illustrations
by Elliott and Barbara Gordon (128 pages, 8 X 10", $16.95)

How to Shoot Stock Photos that Sell
by Michal Heron (192 pages, 8 X 10", $16.95)

Legal Guide for the Visual Artist
by Tad Crawford (224 pages, 7 X 12", $18.95)

Licensing Art and Design by Caryn Leland (112 pages, 6 X 9", $12.95)

Make It Legal by Lee Wilson (272 pages, 6 X 9", $18.95)

Please write to request our free catalog. If you wish to order a book, send your check or money order to Allworth Press, 10 East 23rd Street, Suite 400, New York, New York 10010. To pay for shipping and handling, include $2.50 for the first book ordered and $.50 for each additional book ($5 plus $.50 if the order is from Canada). New York State residents must add sales tax.